connexions

a series of topic books for students in schools and colleges of further education

Ray Jenkins

The lawbreakers

revised edition

General Editor
Richard Mabey
Designer
Arthur Lockwood

Penguin Books Ltd,
Harmondsworth, Middlesex, England
Penguin Books Inc,
7110 Ambassador Road,
Baltimore, Md 21207, U.S.A.
Penguin Books Australia Ltd,
Ringwood, Victoria, Australia

First published 1969
Reprinted 1970
Revised edition 1971
Reprinted 1973
Copyright © Ray Jenkins, 1969, 1971

Made and printed in Great Britain by
Jarrold & Sons Ltd
Set in Lumitype Univers and Clarendon

Alan

The room was intensely quiet. Outside, under the still lime trees,
a youth in white shirt and grey shorts levelled out disturbed pebbles.
The Police had gone. Inside, the ten-year-old boy bit back his tears
and blinked at the superintendent. Mr Bass seemed tall. Immense.

Bass You understand, I've got to write down some things
about you. Your name now?

Alan Alan. Alunwhite.

Bass Religion? *(no reply)* Anything in your pockets?
Handkerchief? Pencil? Money?

Alan No.

Bass Colour of eyes — blue. Scars? Have you ever had an
operation, Alan?

Alan *(showing a wet chin)* Cut me chin on some steps.

Bass Any bullet wounds? Do you wet the bed at all?

Alan No.

Bass Now, let's write down what you're wearing. Canvas
shoes, are those stockings or socks? Underpants?
(Alan nods) Shorts, T-shirt, anorak.

Alan It's gotta hood.

Bass So it has. Do you smoke?

Alan Yes.

Bass How many a day? *(pause)*

Alan Not generally.

Bass Right — now I want you to sign here.

Alan Me whole name?

Bass Like you do your cheques.

Bass You see your number's thirty. It's not because we don't
like your name — it's just a way of keeping your
toothbrush and your towel apart from somebody else's.
A Remand Home's not a prison — it's a home. Now
you tell me why you're here.

Alan Pinching.

Bass Where?

Alan At the Home.

Bass How many Homes have you been to, Alan?

Alan Two.

Bass Didn't you like it there?

Alan They said I tried to kill 'em. But I didn't!

Bass How?

Alan Turning on the gas. But I didn't!

Bass How much did you steal?

Alan Ten quid.

Bass Do you think it right to steal? Do you think it's fair or unfair to be brought here? *(pause)*

Alan Fair.

Bass If you had one wish, Alan, one wish – what would you wish? *(pause)*

Alan A real wish?

Bass Yes.

Alan Go home.

The boy is led off for his bath, his change of clothes and his issue of towel and toothbrush. His clothes will be laundered and ironed and at 9.30 the following morning he will be collected by the Police for attendance at a juvenile court.

Seeing that I feel sorry for him, Mr Bass passes me the committal document. The boy's there under section 32 of the Children and Young Persons Act, 1933, and section 28 of the Children and Young Persons Act, 1969. His offence is stealing (three cases). His character – 'Dishonest and untruthful. Has been cautioned by Police for crime.' His record – 'In the past was often away from home and committed crime. Was beyond parental control and placed in care of local authority. Continually absconded and committed crime. Is very intelligent.' Signed by the officer in case, Detective Constable Wright (778).

The lot of the young offender: transportation in the eighteenth century; prison dinners in the nineteenth.

According to age

Until the middle of last century there was no special provision for the trial of children like Alan: he would have been tried at assizes or quarter sessions like an adult. Indeed, at some earlier time, had he been really unlucky and stolen a loaf of bread, he might have been hanged. It was not until 1908 that prison for children was abolished and they could be treated differently from adults. Now, under the Children and Young Persons Act, 1933–1969, things are different. Even in that short interview some of the benefits are noticeable: and some of the problems.

If Alan had been under ten he would have been deemed incapable of committing a crime. But because he is ten and under fourteen he is regarded as capable and is called a 'child'. If he had been over fourteen and under seventeen he would be a 'young person'. He will now go before a juvenile court — whose special circumstances and rules of procedure we'll look at later. The fact that he has been detained in a remand home and not locked up is vital because the remand home is also an observation centre from which reports are supplied to help the court in deciding the best course to adopt for the welfare of the child or young person. The word 'welfare' is crucial too — because the Act states quite firmly:

'Every court in dealing with a child or young person who is brought before it, either as being in need of care or protection or as an offender or otherwise, shall have regard to the welfare of the child or young person and shall in a proper case take steps for removing him from undesirable surroundings, and for securing that proper provision is made for his education and training.'

One boy in three says he stole

About one London boy in eight between the ages of 13 and 16 admit having been caught by the police for stealing at some time, according to a survey supported by the Home Office and reported by Dr. William Belson, director of the Survey Research Centre of the London School of Economics.

Of the 1,400 boys in the survey, one in three said that they had been caught by someone other than the police. Of the boys who stole, one in four stole from work, one in three stole from relatives, and one in 20 stole motor vehicles.

Two in three said they had entered somewhere without paying for admission ; one in seven said they had threatened others for gain.

Dr. Belson said that although theft tended to increase with each step down the social scale there was still a substantial amount of it among the sons of professional, semi-professional and managerial men.

A most surprising finding was that sons of unskilled workers stole somewhat less than those whose fathers were semi-skilled workers.

'Children and Young Persons'

The Children and Young Persons Act, 1969, extended the idea of 'welfare' to an even greater degree because, basically, the Act, by replacing probation with supervision, by substituting the old harsh divisions of remand, approved school and care of a fit person with the idea of 'community homes' and care of local authority, puts more of the responsibility in helping children and young people in trouble on to social workers, and removes that responsibility from the Courts. The Act fundamentally proposes two things: a. it will raise the minimum age for prosecution from 10 to 14 in stages by order of the Home Secretary (ie a child is still capable of a criminal act under the law, but the consequences will no longer be prosecution); and b. *wherever possible, it replaces prosecutions with care proceedings.* e.g. Section 4 of the Act states 'A person shall not be charged with an offence, except homicide, by reason of anything done or committed while he was a child.'

James Callaghan, the former Home Secretary, regarded the Act as preventing 'the deprived and delinquent children of today from becoming the deprived, inadequate, unstable or criminal citizens of tomorrow.'

On the other hand many magistrates for example resist the Act precisely because it takes the decision making away from the public court and puts it into an uncontrollable area where police, social workers, parents and sometimes schoolteachers bargain over whether a child should be brought before a Court.

What do you think?
Find out what the situation was like before 1969 and what the new proposals mean: read *Children in Trouble* (Cmnd 3601 and make up your own mind.

One day you will have children . . . .

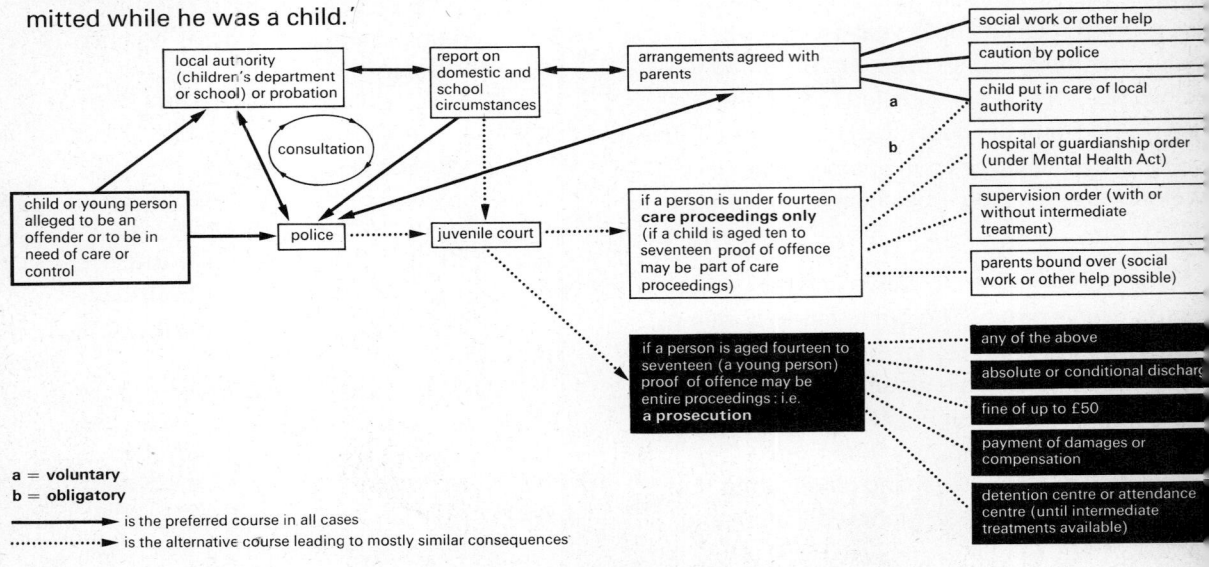

a = voluntary
b = obligatory

——————▶ is the preferred course in all cases

············▶ is the alternative course leading to mostly similar consequences

Has this gone forever?

Talking point

Opinions differ very widely over the wisdom of the Act. Some, like Baroness Wootton of Abinger, welcome it ('In twenty or thirty years time there will be another Bill, and it will be a better one: it will be a Bill to abolish the Juvenile Courts.'); they argue that appearing before a court is a mark for life, it may be deeply upsetting for the juvenile, and it involves fixed legal decisions in a situation which should be very human and flexible. Do you agree?

7

The first offence of a 15-year-old boy

Took stick to match—three months

By Phillip Knightley

THE HOME Secretary is to be asked to examine the case of a 15-year-old boy from Colliers Wood, South London, who is serving three months in Send Detention Centre, Surrey, for taking a stick painted with Chelsea colours into Tottenham football ground last November. It was the boy's first offence.

Police arrested the boy soon after he passed through the turnstiles and charged him with possessing an offensive weapon —the stick. He was convicted at Tottenham Juvenile Court on November 22 without any evidence being heard as to his character and previous behaviour. With juvenile of a serious nature for the such

It was at Tottenham police station that the father, a leading stoker, was told by the duty officer that his son was one of 22 boys aged between 12 and 16 who had been arrested at the match. He showed him a table covered with items which had been taken from them. They included a meat hook, a strap from a Tube filled with sand, and the stick into the ground a walking and which "Ch pl

and then drop it and deny all knowledge of it." He sentenced him to three months in a detention centre. An application for bail pending an appeal refused

The

Youth strangled girl who teased him

SIXTEEN - YEAR - OLD Pauline Dukes teased a youth about his 14-year-old girl friend.

And in a rage he turned on her and strangled her, a judge was told at Kent Assizes yesterday.

Afterwards, 17-year-old Peter Free wrote: " The memory of what I have done will haunt me all my life. I never planned it—

it just happened so quickly."

Free, of Chilham-road, Gillingham, Kent, was sentenced to be detained indefinitely for murdering Pauline, of Grange-road, Gillingham, in a wood near her home on May 12.

WITNESS JAILED—BORSTAL BOYS GET NEW HEARING

Britain's youngest publican, aged 19

CHERYL BROOK yesterday became Britain's youngest publican—just two weeks after her 19th birthday.

Magistrates at Wilmslow, Cheshire, granted her the licence of the Swan Inn, the free house she inherited three years ago at Kettleshulme,

TWO YOUTHS convicted on robbery charges are to have their cases heard again—although previous appeals have been dismissed.

The youths were sent for borstal training for robbing John Phillips, a 22-year-old booking clerk at Chessington South railway station, Surrey, of £63.

One of the youths, John Hobbs, of Wimbledon, admitted stealing some of the money, but denied stealing the whole amount.

The other, Lee Jones, of Chessington, denied being at the station when the robbery took place. Hobbs backed up his story.

Then last November Phillips was jailed for 15 months at South West London Sessions for falsifying ticket entries and embezzlement at the station, setting fire to books and documents to destroy records, and theft. He asked for 32 other offences to be taken into consideration.

By SIDNEY WILLIAMS

sacked after his conviction, has moved from Battersea and cannot be found.

The parents of both youths, who are still being kept in borstal, have been told about the appeals.

One of them, Mrs. Katharine Jones, said last night: "I first wrote to the Home Secretary about this in August when I learned that Phillips had been arrested.

"The Home Office have written to me saying they regret the delay in replying—seven months—and telling me about this appeal.

What is law?

The scream of crime headlines constantly reminds us that law exists. It is one of the nerves of our society and, like Alan, we probably first notice it when we brush up against it — and are caught! But, whether we agree to it or not, our waking, sleeping, home and public life are covered by it. Objects as well as people represent law — traffic lights, yellow lines, rate demands, grilles over jewellers' windows, the 'A', 'AA', 'U' and 'X' certificates attached to films. Law watches us grow up:

'Under 5   no intoxicants — by law (except "in case of sickness").

Over 5   off to school.

Under 10   cannot commit a crime. However bad the deed, it *cannot* be criminal.

Under 12   must not be left in a room with an unguarded fire.

Under 13   mustn't be sold fireworks; and mustn't drive tractors on a farm.

Under 14   mustn't be allowed to pawn anything. Mustn't be in the bar of a pub during "opening hours".

Under 15   cannot leave school. Cannot be fostered (for payment) by anyone not registered with the local authority.

Under 16   cannot marry. Mustn't be sold cigarettes or tobacco.

These go on and on. But from sixteen to twenty-one the restrictions get complicated by exceptions. The "infant" is now growing up fast: the law has to be a little less grandmotherly — especially about drinking in pubs. A teenager who can understand *exactly* what the law intends about the occasions when he can drink in pubs until he is eighteen should take up the law as a profession.'

From *The Law is Yours* by C. H. Rolph

Definition

As an easy definition, Law is a set of rules to preserve ORDER, resolve CONFLICT, and KEEP THE PEACE.

Through statutes, acts of parliament and the accumulated opinions of judges over a long period of time, law predicts possible troubles — so that when an offence takes place, there's a rule to cover it. As in football, everybody agrees to the rules and the game takes place. If there is a disagreement, society has appointed an interpreter of the rules — a referee, a magistrate, a judge — and he attempts to reach a solution.

In exchange for doing exactly what we like we agree to laws, otherwise there would be chaos! If we didn't, every single disagreement would have to be solved by the two people concerned and, dangerously, only the strongest, or the biggest, or the most influential would survive; the law of the jungle would prevail — 'red in tooth and claw'.

Primitive law

The fact that Alan will be tried, not by the *cook* he stole from, but by an *independent* judge representing the state, has its roots in **primitive law.**

In early society, the *tribe* or *clan*, in the interests of everybody, acted as the judge between two quarrellers. But, as the societies developed, this right to judge and impose punishment shifted over to *officials* representing the general society: this *sub-tribe* became dominant and usually consisted of the *chiefs*. The Chief or King represented the whole of society and, in criminal matters, offences came to be seen, not as private wrongs, but as offences against the King: they were breaches of the *King's Peace*. The scope of royal courts became wide and penetrating. In this way the *law* and its *officers* evolved as the third party in any dispute between King and subject, or subject and subject. In Alan's case the third voice between him and the cook is the *magistrate* and the juvenile court.

Alan would not have been punished for theft in a primitive court because food and tools tended to be shared by everybody. Nor would he have been imprisoned because it was regarded as too troublesome. Imprisonment is the invention of 'civilized' law! The punishment for continual anti-social behaviour was exile or death, but, gradually, the idea of *fines* or *damages* became a method of settlement — a solution most courts throughout the world still use.

A return to primitive law — a clip from the film of *Lord of the Flies*.

The oldest Greek trial of which we have record was one arising out of a dispute between a 'slayer' and an 'avenger' as to who should receive or not receive the blood-money. The hearing was held publicly and was attended by friends of both contestants who were kept in order by public officers (heralds). The 'daysman' or judge was supported by the elders. They sat 'on polished stones in the sacred circle', and in the middle lay two pieces of gold to be awarded either to the party who made out the best case — or to the elder who could provide the best rule of law governing the case.

There are at least five basic features of a modern court case traceable in that trial — can you name them?
Answers on page 33

Common law

By its very nature primitive law was not written down and in this sense it is an example of what we call **common law**. Common law has grown slowly out of the decisions made by judges from earliest times which were often reached in the light of the local customs and unwritten rules of their society. When written down these decisions became accepted laws until they were altered to meet new circumstances. Some of the ancient common law is written into Acts of Parliament, but much remains unwritten.

Statute law is different in that it is written and laid down by the authority of Parliament and has to be followed by the judges exactly as it is written — the Factory, Health and Education Acts are examples of this. But in spite of the incredible bulk of Statute law — our Statutes began with the reissue of Magna Carta in the thirteenth century — the most basic part of our law is still common law. No statute, for instance, lays it down in general terms that a man *must* pay his debts, or honour his contracts, or pay damages for trespass, or libel or slander: common law assumes this.

So that when we speak of **the law** we are thinking of law which includes both statute and common law — and perhaps more of the latter than the former.

It is important to realize that, although at first sight it might seem slightly laughable that a learned and intelligent judge spends time deciding over very small particulars, the outcome might be vital.

His decision will set a *precedent* — and other cases will be decided in the light of it. Our system is rich because the judges are guided, not by theory, but by the millions of difficulties that have arisen in real life and been dealt with and become guidelines for the future. **But . . . can you see any disadvantages in a system which is based on previous cases?**

Between the law and the offender comes another 'authority' — the police.

Statutes and Acts of Parliament are not merely a succession of 'don'ts'. If society has to be protected from the individual, the individual also has the right to be protected from society!

Did you know that:

1 Under the 1965 Rent Act where harassment or illegal eviction is threatened, the tenant can complain to the local authority whose job it is to take an action on his behalf?
2 For debts under £50, the debtor can go to court and avoid bankruptcy by getting an administration order? Sections 148–56, County Courts Act, 1959
3 Under the Education Act, 1944, parents have a right to influence the choice of school for their children?
4 If an employee thinks he has been wrongfully dismissed, he can sue his employer?
5 There are rent tribunals, industrial tribunals and mental health review tribunals at a citizen's disposal?

Can you find any examples from newspapers or elsewhere to question whether these rights are upheld in every case?

The police

The Charlie

Originally parish constables, their duties had included enforcing the magistrate's decisions on matters like eviction for rent arrears, flogging tramps and clamping people in the stocks.

By the eighteenth century they were a standing joke. In the fashionable parts of London, the charlie had his box at the end of the road (much like a present day sentry box), where he could hide at the first sign of trouble.

'A friend of mine couldn't sleep at all. His physicians put him on an experiment. They dressed him in a watchman's coat, put a lantern in his hand and placed him in a sentry box and in ten minutes he was asleep.'

Because of such inefficiency, the authorities relied increasingly on savage punishments to deter people.

The Bow Street Runner

These men were known in the eighteenth century as 'robin-redbreasts' — from the scarlet waistcoats they wore under their blue frock coats. In addition to their uniforms they were supplied with a small hollow wooden baton called a tipstaff. This was partly a weapon and partly a means of carrying a warrant of arrest. They also carried a pair of handcuffs and a pistol.

Their honesty, physical strength and perseverance soon made them the terror of the gangs. They patrolled the streets by night as well as by day, and were the first detectives in our sense of the word — one of their duties being to solve crimes. In order to do this they maintained close contact with the criminal underworld. The Runners were paid a regular one guinea a week and their first duty was to the Bow Street Magistrate — but they were often asked to solve crimes as far away as Glasgow — and their services could be hired for a guinea a day.

Even today a citizen can hire a P.C. for £1.84 an hour for a private function, or a dog for 95p a day.

Look up the following names in a good encyclopedia and find out why they are important in the history of the police. Henry Fielding, Sir Robert Peel, Cesare Lombroso, Alphonse Bertillon, Alfred Stratton, Dr Hawley Harvey Crippen.

The Peeler

An organized Police Force began to take shape in England after Sir Robert Peel's Police Bill, 1829. The Peelers or Bobbies were the first policemen to be employed full-time at a regular wage (£50 a year). Education was not considered necessary.

They wore a blue high-collared frock coat reaching to just above the knee with eight large brass buttons, a leather belt, brass buckle and blue trousers. The high collar was fastened in such a way that it made it almost impossible for the Peeler to turn his head! The chimney-pot hat had a metal frame — partly to protect his head from attack and partly to stand on to look over walls. They carried a rattle to call for help (replaced in 1880 by a whistle), a baton marked 'police officer' and a striped armlet when on duty. They were not detectives but preventers of crime — and within a year or so their vigilance had driven many criminals to places like Liverpool where 240,000 townspeople had no police body at all except for a few elderly night watchmen.

The Modern Copper

In 1962 we spent £130 million on 87,432 police employees in England and Wales; the American Federal Bureau of Investigation in 1964 spent $147 million on only 14,000 employees. The modern copper is taught to cultivate the co-operation of the public by 'combining modesty and firmness, and dignity of manner and address, with good humour and kindly friendliness and by showing infinite patience under provocation'. Many policemen originate from lower social and economic groups but soon acquire middle-class standards of obedience, cleanliness and punctuality which are built into the Police Disciplinary Code. But, as a result of Parliament having made him an all-purpose public servant, he is still, in a highly technical society, expected to act as judge, social worker, lawyer and doctor without training as any of them. Despite the high mobility of some criminals, much value is still placed on local know-how which finds expression in motorized patrols working alongside men actually living on the beat.

Statement...

For most people 'The Law' means the police, magistrates' courts and county courts. Respect for law and confidence in the system depends very much on the conduct of cases in the courts, and on the behaviour of the police.

The policeman is *not* the law. If he isn't — why not get a policeman to come to your school and explain *what* he is? In the meantime jot down *your* ideas of what he is — and then read the following extracts from a long interview with a policeman of nearly twenty years' experience. The notes on pages 16–17 have been added after the interview:

1 . . . To start with — a copper expects to be hurt — not physically but mentally — because he's doing the job he's doing . . .

2 . . . Look at the strains on a young copper — he's 19, he's a normal chap who suddenly becomes a policeman; his contemporaries, the mates he went to school with, who are now in other jobs — clerks, mechanics, whatever — they can do what they like, say what they like: he can't . . .

3 . . . The professional code makes it hard for him to make any distinction between his private and his public life: he's a copper twenty-four hours a day, and people expect him to be; he's a public servant . . .

4 . . . Under the Police Act, 1964, any written complaint about a policeman — even if it's that his dog has run on the next door neighbour's lawn — has to be dealt with to the satisfaction of the person complaining; yes, it's true he's dealt with by the police themselves — but where his superiors might overlook minor disciplinary offences (being late), where the public's concerned they've got to look at it: a guilty copper is letting the job down . . .

5 . . . He's not a machine — he's even probably a bit more red-blooded than the rest — he's a Minister of the Crown — impartial, responsible for his actions, in law, to himself. No superior officer can tell another copper — 'arrest that man': he's responsible, alone, for his actions . . .

6 . . . Yes, I think he is 'a little bit different from other people'. His sternness for example is probably the result of his consciousness of his own responsibility — yes, and it may be a worry of making mistakes. Remember this — people go to him — even if a judge and an M.P. have a car collision — it's the copper who sorts it out, who's looked to as the authority for that moment; even without a lot of experience of life he could be called in to sort out a vicious quarrel between a man and his wife, or a landlord and a tenant, or a coloured row . . .

7 . . . Incidentally the kind of copper we jump on is the 'know-all': not because he's clued up, no, but he's just not the type the public expects . . .

8 . . . We're killjoys — on the one hand we're taught 'not to interfere with the innocent pursuits of the public' — yet on the other hand, if a copper does his duty, it's impossible at some time *not* to upset people. For example? Couples in door-ways — of course they might be innocent, but they might be there for another purpose; coppers are there, remember, for the prevention of crime . . .

9 . . . Unlike a bank clerk, he needs his self-discipline *as a policeman* to help him in positions where his normality would get in the way — for example — arresting a meths drinker, dealing with children who have been savagely hurt, or taking

'I could see the bullet hit him in the head. He wasn't
worried about the gun. He still fought like a maniac'

HOW A DETECTIVE DIED: ALLEGED STATEMENT

'THE DEATH OF A BRAVE BASTARD'

DET.-CONSTABLE IAN COWARD

By KENNETH TEW
OXFORD, Monday.

AN UNARMED detective fatally shot
in the street was described as a
"brave bastard" by the man who
killed him, a court was told today.

The prosecution at Oxford Assizes
produced an alleged statement by Arthur
William Skingle, 25, one of two men accused
of murdering at Reading Detective-constable
Ian Coward, married with one son.

Skingle's statement—seven written foolscap pages
—was read by the Clerk of Assize, Mr. William Lewis.

The statement said : "I took the revolver from my
waistband and pointed it at him. I said, 'Don't move
and nothing will happen.'

"He dropped one bit of the radio and struck at
the gun with the other and tried to grab the gun with
his other hand.

control of a particularly terrible traffic accident. He
has to do his crying when he's finished . . .

10 . . . The bulk of his training goes towards
teaching him to use his *discretion.* Don't forget any
man who can tell another man to do something has
power. Of course he has to learn to use this properly
— under the Metropolitan Police Act, 1839, it is an
offence to shake a mat on to a public thoroughfare
other than a doormat before 8 a.m. . . . mother can
be arrested for this, or her kids for bowling hoops!
What if he prosecuted everybody under the Litter Act!
But if on the other hand the copper sees someone
begging — and uses his discretion to the degree of not
arresting — he himself is liable to a financial penalty . . .

11 . . . Policemen are not allowed to express
political opinions . . . of course they come to be asso-
ciated with the establishment because they are the
establishment. If you're talking about demonstrations
and Tariq Ali, you have to remember the police have to
represent order . . . the extreme left wing (and don't
forget the right wing only love us if we don't interfere
with them!) are and always have been against the
public order — they believe in revolution. Tariq Ali may
want to demonstrate peaceably — I believe he does —
but he can't guarantee that some extreme fringe won't

want to make trouble. In other words he can't
guarantee the *other* factions, the others who want to
break his lot up. Oswald Mosley might have wanted
to hold a peaceful demonstration, but because he's
who he is he attracts hatred. In the middle of this
who keeps the Queen's Peace? Perhaps policemen
don't like bolts in their eyes — but they're still expected to show forbearance . . .

12 . . . I suppose a copper's politics are somewhere in the middle — mauvey-pink. But in the case
of civil disturbance he doesn't care who he uses
his force against; he leaves his politics behind. You
don't know sometimes who you've arrested, as long
as you've arrested them properly, as long as you've
preserved the peace. Yes, they may get angry, but
never biased. They can't afford to be biased . . .

13 . . . The drawbacks? The young copper may
not like communal life — and he has to live in a
section house if he's a bachelor; he may not like
shift work, he'll get frustrated on the restrictions on
his private life . . . and there's the unpleasant functions I've spoken of . . .

14 . . . The advantages — the uniform: he
doesn't have to be *doing* anything — the fact that
he's in uniform walking down the street means he's
preventing crime. Then there's the status in the
community — job-satisfaction — the rewards of the
job are immediate: there's immediate satisfaction in
having done something worthwhile — which some
people in other jobs have to wait long-term to feel . . .

15

... and comment

1 Hitting a policeman with spaghetti is an offence in Italy, described as 'outraging a public official'. A copper could be hurt mentally at the thought of limited chances of promotion – 80 per cent are constables, 12 per cent sergeants, and therefore only 8 per cent attain senior rank.

2 Seventy-four per cent of the county policemen and 44 per cent of the city men think they would have more friends if they had a different job.

3 'There is a further not inconsiderable disadvantage in police work, and this is the burden of social isolation that the police feel their position carries. This isolation is experienced . . . to some extent by their wives and children as well. It follows that the police are continually in a defensive position and any real or imagined criticism from individuals or sections of the general public, press, or authorities such as the courts or M.P.s is liable to produce in the police mind a distorted impression of what the public in general feel about them.'
Social Survey, Central Office of Information, 1960

4 Despite his position, a policeman remains a member of the public; for example, when chasing criminals the police driver may exceed the speed limit, but he is liable for an accident in the same way as a private driver and can be prosecuted for dangerous driving.

5 The working class has always been somewhat hostile to the police. Do you think this is still true? If you were a long-haired owner of a noisy twin-stroke would you be addressed 'Excuse me, sir'? Or would a copper say 'Hey you!' to the pin-striped owner of a Rolls? Does class come into it? A countess is apologized to for a raid on her flat for drugs; a pop group, raided in the same way, received no apology. Impartial?

6 Sheffield and Thurso apart, the public seldom accuses the police of corruption. (At least things are not so bad as in Spain where people who accused the police of misconduct in 1963 were charged with military rebellion!) The police, and especially the Criminal Investigation Department, work close to the criminal world. Temptation probably comes more frequently in their work than to anybody else in society. 'We demand that a good detective will be adept at bribing and blackmailing informers on our behalf, but never on his own. He often knows as well that the man who tries to bribe him has no moral right to the money he is offering. The opportunities are so great that the police are expected to be above suspicion: there are Draconian penalties for any default (though the maximum penalty for theft by a police officer is not so high as it is for a postman).'
From *The Police* by Ben Whitaker

It is the same with using violence. No member of the public can expect an unarmed policeman to tackle an armed criminal without using force; and a police officer who fails to make an arrest or allows an escape is liable to find himself on a serious disciplinary charge.

7 What exactly does 'the public expect'? Have TV programmes like 'No Hiding Place', 'Z-Cars', 'Softly Softly' and 'Dixon of Dock Green' altered your view?

8 The police of course don't make the rules: the power resides elsewhere to make us do and conform. But if they didn't enforce the law, or were seen not to believe in it, then the law and order itself would all into disrepute. Do you believe, for example, that policemen, let alone the majority of the public, believe in the abortion laws, Sunday observance of the licensing laws? Do they always have to behave as if they do?

9 The one hatred shared by most coppers is for sexual offences against children. The copper who had an almost manic crusade against insanitary hot-dog stalls tended to be the exception!

10 The Cheshire M6 police say they give *verbal* warnings to nine out of ten motorists they stop.

Homosexuality is now among the 9 per cent of offences over which *no one* in the police has any discretion at all. Gone are the days when policemen hid in toilets to try and obtain evidence. Homosexuality, together with murder, incest, rape and race relations offences, is, for the sake of uniformity, referred to the Director of Public Prosecutions. This, in part, relieves some policemen from having to spend time in court as prosecutors.

11 The fact that policemen are not allowed to express political opinions adds to the impression, especially among students, that they're for 'Them' and against 'Us'. Where would the police stand in the event of civil war?

'Today it is difficult to believe that such a thing as a police strike could ever have happened in English history. But in 1872 and 1890 some of the police went on strike for more pay, and in 1918 about 6000 and in 1919, 2400 men came out asking for recognition of their union. In 1926 the police refused to join the General Strike, although their situation was not an easy one and their feelings must have been mixed during some incidents. Afterwards *The Times* collected a public subscription of £242,000 in gratitude — "A gargantuan tip" in the words of one chief inspector — but some policemen disliked it because it came from the upper classes and impugned their impartiality; and they wrote to the *Police Review* suggesting it should be given to the people who needed it.'

From *The Police* by Ben Whitaker

12 At present there is no formal right to any compensation for damage or injury suffered by somebody helping the police, but application for compensation for physical injury can be made to the Criminal Injuries Compensation Board.

13 Central area policemen, where crime is at its most intense, tend to be bachelor and young: the more mature, married men want the peace of the suburbs. Is this fact significant?

14 The deterrent effect of uniforms has been studied on the Continent — the stationing of a gendarme at a blind corner has been shown to reduce accidents, and in Paris, 1959, when many police were in Algeria, they even placed cut-out dummies at dangerous cross-roads with great success!

'No' to false policemen

A PLAN by French police to place wooden models of Gendarmes at accident black spots to try and curb road accidents has been described as "impractical" for London.

"It wouldn't work in the Metropolitan Police District," says Commander Harry Crowden of Traffic Division.

"The dummies would be excellent trophies. I think we would lose them all."

999 driver blamed

A police driver answering a 999 call in a police Jaguar car was "entirely to blame" for another driver's death, a High Court judge ruled yesterday. Police drivers could not be criticised for fast driving in such emergencies, but they must not drive at such speeds that they lost control, said Mr Justice Beam.

He awarded Mrs Patricia Mary McLeod, aged 36, of Coleshill Flats, Ebury Street, London, £15,719 damages and costs for the death of her husband.

Not all, but 2400 police came out on strike in 1919.

From the figures below – do you think there is any relation between the *numbers of police* and the *discouragement of crime?*

Town	Policemen per 100,000 people	Crime clear-up rate
Leicester	163	50·7%
Sunderland	144	49·5%
Dewsbury	170	53·7%
Cambridgeshire	156	53·8%
Wiltshire	120	46·7%
Lancashire	143	48·6%

Talking point

If you were a Chief Constable – would you first:

1 Spend more money on technical aids – such as closed-circuit TV, radar, motorized policemen
2 Lower the height qualification of 5 feet 8 inches for men entering the force
3 Advocate a *national* police force
4 Take more trouble in educating the public

in your fight against mounting crime figures?

'OK, knock it off, Marshal Dillon—
that's not the purpose of firearm
training for the police.'

To most of us, the police are the visible
symbols of Law, Order, the Power of
Authority and all that stuff. This being
so it is perhaps unfortunate that police
uniforms throughout the world would
seem to be expressly designed to make
the wearer look ridiculous.

It is in the symbolic context that
police usually appear in my drawings.
Sometimes they are drawn
sympathetically, sometimes less so.
Justice is blindfold. My policemen
often wear their helmets over their
eyes.

Keith Waite

Keith Waite

Osbert Lancaster

'Archdeacon or no archdeacon, a
doctor of divinity still ain't a
doctor within the meaning of
the Act.'

19

Meet Polly

Name:	Pauline Waters
Age:	fourteen years, three months
School:	girls' grammar
Offence:	stealing from an Oxford Street store, two cardigans and a pair of tights: value £4.70
Place of trial:	juvenile court

By stealing Polly has broken the law, been arrested by the police and prosecuted by another citizen (the store manager) for committing a crime.

Alan, probably, is a special case and because of his home background, etc., is likely to belong to that small class of persistent offenders despite efforts by everybody concerned. On this occasion he was committed for approved school training. As the superintendent, Mr Bass, wrote to me:

'It is so sad, you will agree, but we must remember that he *was* a menace to society. At ten years of age he may well respond to training and make the grade when he eventually returns to society. Everything of course will depend on the home background and the support he will receive in the home setting.'

But what about somebody like Polly – the first offender. Will she join the 70 per cent of people who come before a court and don't reappear? We'll follow her case through, but first *what is a crime?*

What is a crime?

English law is divided into two main sections: **criminal law,** which deals largely with offences for which people can be punished and **civil law,** which concerns disputes between two or more people and which usually has nothing to do with the question of punishment.

So, we can give a technical definition of what a crime is:

'Any action or omission, punishable by a penalty, which only the Sovereign in the exercise of the Royal Prerogative of mercy may pardon or remit.'

From *The Criminal Law* by F. T. Giles

But it is much easier, and free from squabble, to say simply —

A crime is an offence punishable in a criminal court.'

In other words the distinction is not between the *acts* but between the legal proceedings. To show how complicated it can be:

'If the driver of a bus drives recklessly and comes into collision with a private car, damaging that car and some of his own passengers, that same act of reckless driving is a crime, also a *tort* (a civil wrong) to his passengers and the owner of the private car, and also a *breach of contract* with the passengers in not using due care and skill in carrying them! If proceedings against the driver are *aimed at punishing him,* then those proceedings are *criminal,* whereas proceedings that *aim at compensating* the injured persons are *civil.*' From *The Machinery of Justice in England* by R. M. Jackson

The truth is (luckily for us) that there's too much law to be enforced. On the day I read that letter I walked from Waterloo Station to Holborn, cocking a special (and once-practised) eye for violations of the Laws of England. I got the following bag:

A girl feeding the pigeons inside Waterloo Station.

Two cars with expired Excise licences.

Three cars with none at all.

Twenty-three cars parked wholly or partly on the footway.

One lorry with its lowered tailboard hiding the rear number plate while in motion.

A furniture van with its rear number chalked on the back.

One flag-day girl shaking a collecting box in people's faces.

One boy throwing a half-eaten egg sandwich into the roadway.

Three shop awnings that you had to duck under.

A cycling window-cleaner carrying a ladder on his shoulders.

And a painter on a window-sill wearing no means of preventing a fall.

I would say it was a typical lot. And among the things too numerous to count were cars bearing advertising 'stickers', vehicles waiting on double yellow lines, and disembarking bus passengers throwing their tickets away.

I've known policemen who would have hated to let any of these escape. They would all have been seen as personal affronts. But even a policeman like that couldn't have coped with more than one of them. If he chose the cycling man with the ladder, who was actually the most dangerous, all the rest would have got away. So perhaps he would have chosen the three shop blinds, on the ground that they might have knocked his helmet off (they ought to be 8ft 6in from the ground).

C. H. Rolph in the *Guardian*

Courts

The opening of the new Law Term. Judges walk in procession to the House of Lords for the traditional breakfast.

Because of her age Polly is to be brought before a juvenile court — which is a magistrates' court specially set up to deal with juvenile delinquents, and, so to speak, is at the foot of the criminal courts' tree.

If she had stolen with someone over seventeen, then she would have been charged jointly and the trial would have taken place in the adult court. But under the Criminal Justice Act, 1948, no court can send a person under twenty-one to prison unless it is of the opinion that no other method of dealing with him is appropriate. In a sense this is an extension of the idea of welfare that we considered in the case of Alan.

Almost all criminal proceedings begin in the magistrates' courts and ninety-seven out of every 100 end in them. But it is as well to remember that criminal law forms but a small part of English law. In a way it is more glamorous, but it is not the whole story.

Fundamental rights

As we saw in our simple definition of law, society, once it sets up laws, also seeks to devise punishments to fit the crimes. But although the court is there to prove the facts of Polly's case, pronounce her sentence, and therefore defend society, it is also careful to protect her rights.

Before she enters the court, Polly will be protected by certain principles which would equally apply if she were older, if she had committed murder, stolen aboard ship two miles off-shore, or simply played truant:

1 She is presumed innocent before she is proved guilty. (Compare France.)

2 The prosecutor must prove the charge he is making against the accused.

3 Proof must be beyond all reasonable doubt.

4 The hearing must be in public (except for juvenile courts and matrimonial proceedings).

5 Witnesses must give their evidence in the presence of the accused, and she must be allowed to question them when they have given their evidence.

6 The court must listen to everything the accused or her lawyers have to say which is relevant to her defence.

7 Once the court comes to a decision whether to acquit or convict, the defendant can never again be charged with that particular offence.

A few days later, nervous but outwardly calm, Polly sits with her mother waiting for her case to be called. Mother's lips tremble and shiver. Polly says — 'It's all right, Mum, I'll get off first time!'

House of Lords

↑ appeal to

**Court of Appeal
(criminal division)**

↑ appeal to

**High Court
Queens Bench
Division**

Crown Court ✱

appeal on
point of law
only

appeal to
committal for trial
committal for sentence

**Magistrates
Court**

✱ replaces Courts of Quarter Session and Assize
Courts Act 1971

A Juvenile Court

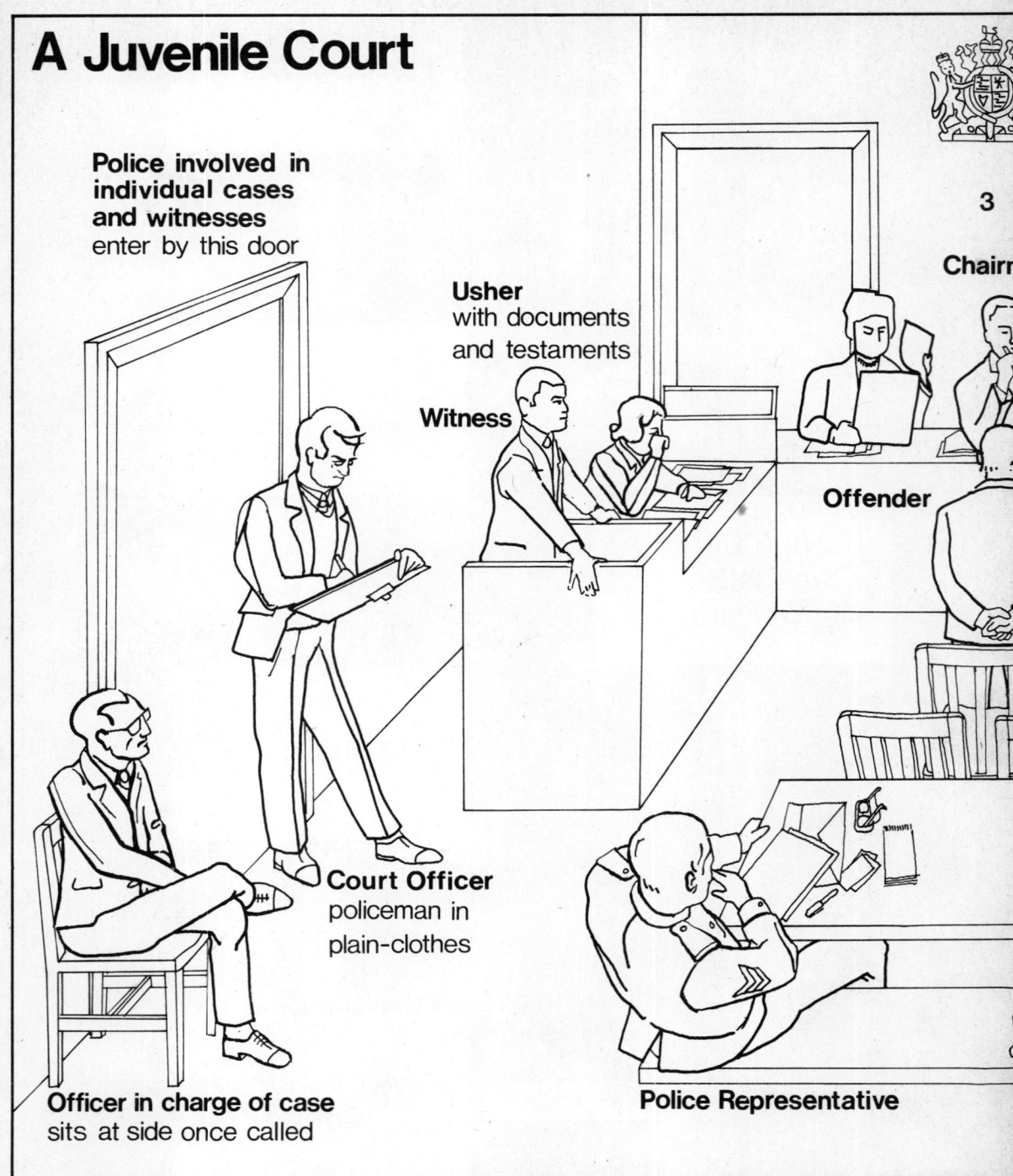

Police involved in individual cases and witnesses enter by this door

Usher with documents and testaments

Witness

3

Chairm

Offender

Court Officer policeman in plain-clothes

Officer in charge of case sits at side once called

Police Representative

Coat of Arms

Two impressions from young offenders:

'There are such a lot of people that is what people get scared of and think they won't get a fair trial'

'I had too much worry on my mind to notice anything'

strates

he must be woman

arents

Clerk to the Justices

Solicitors and Counsel

Probation Officers

Education Department Representatives

Local Authority Social Workers

Press and Visitors sit at back of room

The juvenile court

Although the juvenile court is one type of magistrates' court it must be held separately and preferably in a different room from the ordinary court-room. If an ordinary court-room is used, the juvenile court must not be held within an hour before or after its use for the other court. The hearing and whole atmosphere is less formal, the 'dock' is abolished, the youngster and his parents sit near to the magistrate and on the same level, and there are no court 'furnishings'. In some courts bright curtains line the windows. Police staff the proceedings but they are usually in plain clothes. Legal representatives may appear, but if they don't a parent or guardian may conduct the defence. The court is *not* open to the public and the press cannot print any of the actual names of the offenders or write of them in such a way that they would be identifiable with the offender.

Except in trivial cases the court is required to take into account a number of things affecting the youngster, such as his medical history, home background, school record and any report of the probation officer or local authority. The court must tell the parent or guardian what the court proposes to do and then allow the parent to give his views about the proposed course of action.

As we shall see, it is the chairman of the bench who does most of the talking — but he or she is helped by the Clerk to the Justices, a lawyer who is there not only to give legal advice but also to protect the child's interest: the aim of the court being 'to treat the offender rather than the offence'.

Just as the setting is simplified so is the conduct of the court. The offender, if giving evidence, takes an oath and promises to tell the truth, but this is rare as 99 per cent of those who appear before the court plead guilty. The words 'sentence' and 'conviction' are no longer used. If the real heart of the law is finding the truth by statement, evidence, question and answer, it is certainly here, but in a quieter, more chatty form. In this atmosphere knowing the facts counts just as much as knowing the law.

The scene is set for Case 14.

What does an unusual Clerk to the Justices think of his job, of his role?

'I knew I was a lawyer once I understood that you can use the system to do good. Most lawyers who defend, who are advocates, don't believe in their clients; and I resent being equated with them! The path to success is in prosecution — using the hammer of the state to crack the individual. As a defence lawyer you have to use the framework of the law to the *advantage* of the individual — making the job into as good a thing as it can be!

In the setting of a juvenile court, I find it easy to speak as a lawyer to kids, without having to wrap it up in the mystique of language — which many lawyers adore — just as doctors write their prescriptions in Latin! It's easy to do and one can't help but be tempted by it. Law must be made intelligible to people — you must have laws that can be read!

Seeing someone acquitted: that's my kick! If I can get a case thrown out — I'm as pleased as punch!'

Case 14

The **usher** leads **Polly** and **Mrs Waters** to seats before the magistrate, **Mrs Lyon.**

Usher   This is Polly, your worship, and mother.

(The Chairman nods and Polly and Mrs Waters sit.)

Clerk   Age?

Polly   F-fourteen and a half.

Clerk   Polly, you're charged with stealing two cardigans and a pair of tights from Allied Wholesalers Ltd — do you understand what that means?

Polly   Yes.

Clerk   Do you admit stealing this clothing?

Polly   *(very quiet)* Yes.

Magistrate   Who can give us the facts?
(W.P.C. Rodgers steps into the witness box.)

Rodgers   W.P.C. Rodgers. At 11.35 a.m. on Saturday, 15 June 1968, I was called to Allied Wholesalers Ltd store in Oxford Street by Mr Stevens, the manager, who said to me in Polly's presence, 'This girl has just been caught stealing in the store. I'm fed up, it's the fifteenth loss this week. If it isn't foreign girls, it's our own.' I cautioned her and said, 'What have you to say?' She replied, 'I'm sorry, do you have to tell my parents?'
(pause, W.P.C. Rodgers steps down from the box but stands ready to answer any questions.)

Clerk   Do you want to ask any questions, Polly?
(Polly shakes her head.)

Magistrate   Now, Polly, what's all this about?

Clerk   Stand up.

1   Magistrates are unpaid.

2   Juvenile justices outside London are elected by the justices themselves to serve on the Juvenile Panel. In London they are specially selected by the Lord Chancellor. Does this seem a satisfactory way of recruiting new justices?

3   Most Juvenile Magistrates are women, of a certain class, because only they seem to have the need to do good and have time to spare. There is great difficulty in finding a sufficient quantity of suitable *male* applicants.

4   Magistrates are supposed to sit twenty-six times a year — or once a fortnight.

5   The former Lord Chancellor, Lord Gardiner, wanted to widen the type of class from which magistrates are selected.

6   The retiring age from the Juvenile Bench is sixty-five.

7   The suitable age for first appointment of magistrates is thirty to forty years of age; none are appointed after fifty.

Case 14

Theft of 'status symbols' by girls

Four German schoolgirls who stole from shops while visiting Carnaby Street as part of an educational tour, said when arrested that they could not afford the things they stole but Carnaby Street was so famous that the items would be status symbols in Germany. Police-constable G. Campbell said this at Marlborough Street Magistrates' Court yesterday.

The girls were each fined £10. They admitted through an interpreter that they had stolen from John Stephen's shop and Gear Ltd. articles worth altogether £7, including four " I'm backing Britain " stickers.

Magistrate (*gently*) Come up here.
(*Polly steps close to the Bench.*)
Well?

Polly I meant to pay.

Magistrate Then why didn't you?
(*silence*)
Did you have any money on you at the time?

Mrs Waters I'd given her two pounds —

Magistrate Is that true?

Polly Yes.

Magistrate If you'd only wanted *one* cardigan — you could have bought it — is that right?
(*Polly nods.*)
Then why did you need the extra one?

Polly I didn't.
(*Mrs Waters bursts into tears. The usher approaches with a box of tissues, Mrs Waters takes one and blows her nose noisily.*)

Magistrate Polly, what I don't understand —

Polly (*defiant*) They said it was easy! (*pause*)

Magistrate What?

Polly Going in . . . and . . . taking things.

Magistrate Who are 'they'?

Polly The others. At school. (*defiant*) They've done it.

Magistrate If they go and jump in the river — do *you* have to? You don't strike me as a girl who doesn't know her own mind. Were the others caught?
(*Polly shakes her head.*)

Magistrate And you thought you could do the same. Obviously. Well, all I can say is, this is serious, it's very silly. I don't know *what* made you do it — and you don't seem to be able to tell us! And to have a mother who can give you that amount and then for you to — well — abuse her generosity — what're we to think? Do you think you've done wrong?
(*Polly nods.*)

Now mother.
(Mrs Waters comes to Polly's side before the Bench.)
What've you got to say?

Mrs Waters *(tearful)* She's . . . she's very helpful in the . . . house. We do everything for her.

Magistrate Even to giving her two pounds pocket money?
(Mrs Waters nods vigorously and then bursts into tears again; she is obviously too upset to say anything more.)
You see, Polly, you do this to yourself and that to your mother. Is there a school report?
(An education welfare officer hands round copies of the report to the magistrates. They read the papers.)

Clerk Sit down Polly.
(Polly sits. There is silence apart from the slight rustling of paper and the coming and going of people in the court.)

Magistrate Polly, I'm going to summarize what it says here: 'lately she's been cocky . . . mixing with the wrong element' — well we've had proof of that! . . . 'coming in late'.

Mrs Waters But she leaves on time! I make sure!

Magistrate 'Shirking games . . . a general lack of application.' Do you think this is true?
(Polly nods reluctantly.)
Well — we'd like to know a little more about you Polly. So we're going to ask a probation officer to come and see you and your mother and we want you to talk to her, be honest, and help as much as you can —

Polly *(shocked)* B-but, I thought it would be all over today. First time you get conditional discharge!

Magistrate It doesn't mean because it's your first offence we're going to place you under the supervision of a probation officer — it's just we want a report and you will come back in three weeks' time. Mother, will you stand surety in the sum of £10 for Polly's appearance in three weeks' time?

Case 14

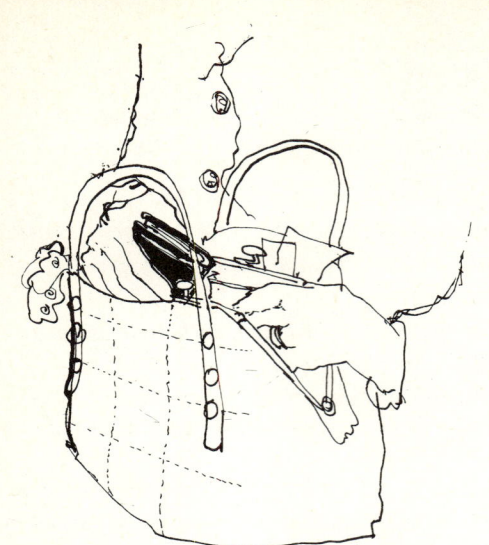

Magistrate *(Mrs Waters nods and fishes in her handbag.)* You don't have to pay now, but if she doesn't turn up you will have to. Now go and talk with the probation officer — and fix up a time to meet. *(Polly and Mrs Waters are ushered from the court.*

Three weeks later Polly reappears in court. Arising out of certain facts in the Social Inquiry Report the magistrates decide to make a Supervision Order (this replaces the old Probation Order). Polly leaves the court. The supervision order is for one year.

Indictable offences: age groups and types of offence, 1970

England and Wales

| | All ages | Under 14 | Age groups | | | |
			14 and under 17	17 and under 21	21 and under 30	30 and over
Number found guilty of indictable offences						
All persons	322,898	23,885	50,512	76,926	86,504	85,071
Females	42,681	2,461	5,356	7,284	10,078	17,502
Males	280,217	21,424	45,156	69,642	76,426	67,569
Percentage of males found guilty of						
Murder or manslaughter	0·1	—	—	0·1	0·1	0·2
Wounding or assault	7·6	1·3	5·1	8·5	9·5	8·2
Other offences of violence	0·2	0·1	—	0·2	0·3	0·3
Sexual offences	2·4	0·7	1·6	1·7	2·2	4·2
Burglary or robbery	24·5	44·6	35·8	26·1	21·3	12·6
Theft or unauthorised taking	51·2	45·4	50·0	53·3	49·7	53·0
Handling stolen goods	7·2	5·8	5·6	5·4	7·8	10·1
Fraud	3·7	0·4	0·7	2·4	5·2	6·6
Other indictable offences	3·1	1·7	1·2	2·3	3·9	4·8
All indictable offences	100·0	100·0	100·0	100·0	100·0	100·0

IN THE INNER LONDON AREA AND IN THE METROPOLITAN POLICE DISTRICT

Before the   Juvenile Court,

of

(hereinafter

called the defendant), who is believed to have been born on

is this day *was on* the   day of   197

found guilty for that   he, on the   day of

197   , at   in the said Area and District, did

Contrary to

It is hereby ordered that the defendant, who resides *will reside* in the County/London Borough/ of

and in the

Petty Sessional Division be placed for the period of   year   from the date of this order under

the supervision of [the Council of the said County/London Borough] [the Council of the County/London

Borough of   who have agreed to be designated as

the supervisor] [a probation officer appointed for or assigned to that Division].

It is further ordered that, for the purpose of facilitating the performance by the supervisor of his duty to

advise, assist and befriend the relevant infant, the relevant infant shall during the said period comply with

the following requirements.

    1.   That   he shall inform the supervisor at once of any change of h   residence or em-

ployment;

    2.   That   he shall keep in touch with the supervisor in accordance with such instructions as may

from time to time be given by the supervisor; and, in particular, that   he shall, if the supervisor so requires,

receive visits from the supervisor at h   home;

[It is further ordered that] [he shall reside with

who has agreed to this requirement].

Dated the   day of   197

Justice of the Peace for the Inner London Area

[*or By order of the Court*

Clerk of the Court].   31

C.Y.P. 43

———

Supervision Order

———

**Criminal
Proceedings**

M.P.-71-84779/5M   M23

What happened to me in court

Polly is fiction – what does it feel like *in fact*?

'. . . I arrived there five minutes early so I was waiting in the waiting room with my parents until I was called, and then as I was entering the court-room I felt all shaky as you are surrounded by people. The judge was a woman about forty. There were a few people sitting in front of her and as she studied my case the clerk started asking her something, and then she left the room for a few minutes, and then she returned, read my case out and explained it to me. And she asked me if I had anything to say. And I said I was sorry – so she give me a fortnight's remand while they went deeper into my case.'

(Sixteen-year-old – conditionally discharged)

'. . . When I was going to court . . . I was so scared. I was walking through the corridors. I heard someone's footsteps coming behind me, a policeman put his hand on my shoulder and said two weeks' remand, you juvenile delinquent.'

(Fifteen-year-old, abandoned by mother at three and seven years old)

'. . . When you get in the court you wait till your name is called out, then you go in. As soon as you get in they start asking awkward questions and when you say a thing they try to twist you out of the words you say. When I went in the policeman who was in charge of my case told a lot of lies. I could not believe it but there you are, a policeman is not a man's friend in any way. The magistrate thinks you're a bit of dirt the way they treat you.'

(Boy, unsatisfactory home)

What do they think of the people in the court!

'. . . too many people, the most I don't like is the newspaper reporters.'

'. . . everyone in the court-room was writing something down.'

And their parents in court?

'. . . When your mother and father does not come with you to court it makes you feel even worse.'

'. . . The court is not very good to the parents of the child.'

What did they think of the magistrates?

'. . . women judges are better – give it me lightly. A man would have said two weeks in Wormwood Scrubs.'

'. . . woman is liable to get sentimental and give short sentences, old-pensioned gentlemen who doesn't like the clothes you wear or long hair give stiff sentences.'

'. . . Some of our sentences depends on your magistrate and your offence. We might think that the magistrate is an old coot but he has his job to do like our mothers and fathers, so it's our own fault if we get into trouble, so there's no one else to blame.'

'. . . The two people on either side of the judge don't seem to take any notice of your case. For instance when I was there one of them was drawing a picture of a horse all the time my case was being heard.'

Answers to page 10.
1 It's *public*.
2 There's a judge (and jury).
3 There are court officials (heralds= police).
4 There is a defendant and a prosecutor.
5 There's the idea of compensation.

They all hated the waiting outside the court.

'. . . waiting and waiting then waiting another hour and a half for the lorry.'

Is the court fair or unfair?

'. . . Unfair! Larceny, one pint of milk. I got a sentence up to my nineteenth birthday. (He is sixteen.) Five weeks before this I stole a motor car and assaulted a policeman with it. For that I only got two years probation, a 10s fine and suspension from driving.'

'. . . They give you years not months like adults . . probation orders are too long.'

'. . . They don't look into it seriously I think it is much better to go to a higher court.'

'. . . I deserve the sentence . . . although I did not think so at the time, the court did its duty yet I don't think I should have got three years.'

'. . . My opinion of the court where I was tried is that the court is a very good and fair court as far as I can see up to now. If we didn't have courts like these, children of nearly all ages would be doing one crime or another so there got (to be) these courts for our own good and protection.'

'. . . I think the court stinks they should think wic about thing it not right sometimes I like to KILL the juge.'

From 'Juvenile courts: The juvenile's point of view', by P. D. Scott, *British Journal of Delinquency*, vol. 9

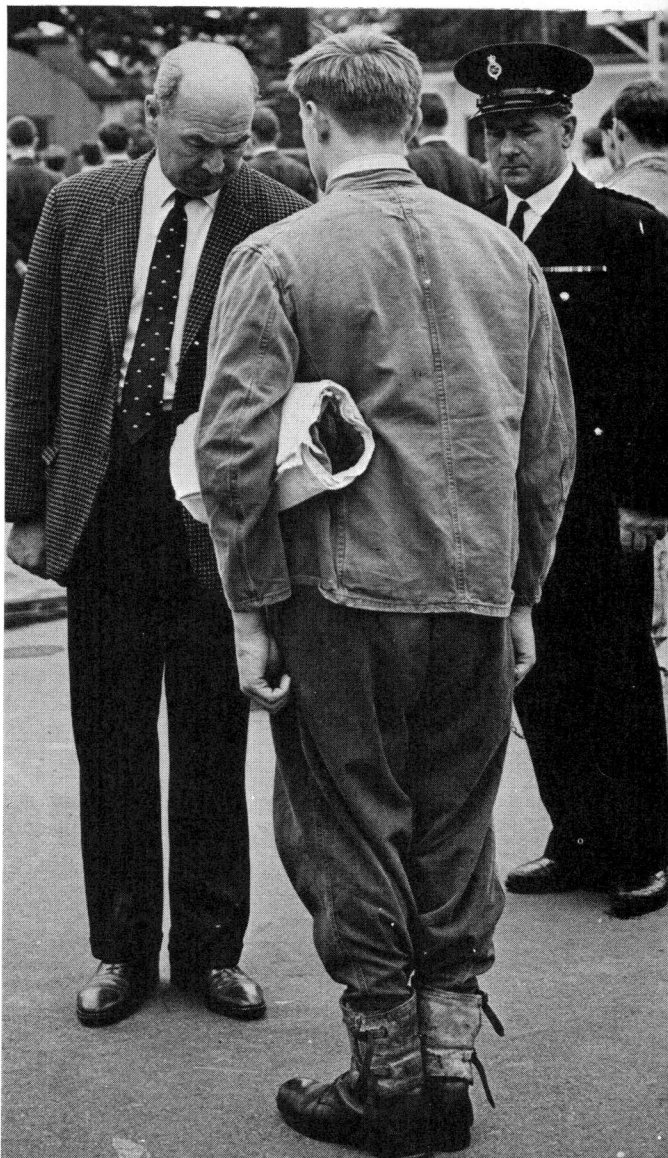

The sequel to the court.

Two sides of the bench

Perhaps the fact that the boys still thought the court 'sentences', that the magistrate was a 'judge', that there was a 'jury', and that the plain-clothes of the policemen in court didn't fool them for a second, means that they see things clearer than we do. We naturally assume that courts are fair, yet behind their heavy, almost theatrical workings, worrying features still exist. Polly and the boys have been tried in a court where the presiding magistrate is *an amateur,* with, until recently, no *direct* training; where evidence is written down by the clerk in *longhand.*

In the higher courts (see page 23) the game of cross-examination sometimes becomes more important than establishing the facts with up-to-date scientific means. Decisions of life and death are left in the hands of inexperienced juries — how can the jurors make up their minds *exactly,* after long hours in a detailed case, without proper notes, or tape recordings of the actual trial? Because, surely, it is important to remember *how* a witness said something as well as remembering *what* he said?

The juvenile court has great legal powers — powers of discharge, probation, detention, fining and committal: powers too great to be misused. What does Mrs Lyon, the magistrate who dealt with Polly, think about it all?

'I think we have a value. I think sometimes we have a sense of proportion. I think we also reflect what society thinks, what the outside people think, which I think is valuable. We aren't so completely bound up in it all — some of the women probation officers get very intense about their cases, and I think that we are more detached and do have a value because of it.`

We'll take up the point about the magistrates 'reflecting what society thinks' later — but if one of the functions of law is *to set right* and, in the case of juveniles, to attach great importance to the welfare side, which *could* involve just sending the offenders to a psychiatrist or child-care officer — is there any *need* for the process of criminal law for this sort of offender?

'Ideally no. I think the value of the courts are that as things are we are the only people that can prosecute and enforce it where necessary. The child must be helped early.'

Mrs Lyon

Apart from regular meals, single beds for probably the first time in their lives and coming out pretty fit, two borstal boys were asked if they were aware that the system was to help?

PRISON officers told yesterday of t
reign of terror by Borstal "bovver boy
that drives their victims to sanctuary—
the punishment block.

Youngsters were so frightened of be
attacked by the thugs that they asked for
tection in the special block.

The fantastic reign of terror and black-mail by Britain's bovver boys was revealed yesterday at the conference of Prison Officers Association.

Mr George Marshall of Rochester, Kent, Borstal told them about the boys at Wellingborough, North-

First boy	They are trying to show you where you've gone wrong and try and help you to go straight again. But what they try to do, I think, is bring all your past up and try and link that in with yourself. If you've had a bad family upbringing they say that's part of it — well I think it is, 'cos I've had a bad upbringing. I think that's what led me to crime. Well, I'm not so sure. That's the impression I got with the people saying this to me. I think they've convinced me that it's me family. But I can never understand. The only time you know you've done wrong is when they've caught you and got you in a cell and you start thinking why you've done it. Then it's too late.
Second boy	If they had longer and tougher borstals like a centre, well I shouldn't think I'd like to do anything like that again. It wouldn't keep me out of trouble but I wouldn't like to be sent down again you see. Just imagine — if I was outside and I saw a house unguarded like I thought I could get in there and get myself three or four hundred pounds for nothing. I wouldn't think to myself, well nobody thinks to themselves 'I'm going to be sent down for this, what will I get?' because you don't think about that. All you're thinking about is what you're going to do with that money when you get the money. You don't think what you're going to get sent down for, or what you are going to get.
First boy	It's not actually being sent to borstal and being in a borstal that worries me, it's the time. I mean this time it's two years, last time it was six months. Next time it could be three even four years, more like a prison sentence. And I don't fancy doing a long 'stretch' as it's called you know. It's just the time that puts you off.
Second boy	I don't think you can be trained not to break and enter. I don't think anybody can even, you know, kind of teach you not to even think about that type of thing I mean. Nobody can teach you to be straight. It's a thing you've got to be on your own.

Is there a criminal type?

'One out of every three males, and one out of every twelve females will be convicted at some time during their life if the conditions now prevailing continue.'
Society influences man. The materialistic, status-conscious world we live in *invites* crime by the open display of an abundance of goods, by the emphasis on acquiring things through pressure of persistent advertising and by the acceptance that material things are a counterpart of status. 'If you haven't *got* things – you're nobody.' Crime cannot alter the rank into which you were born, or get you brains. But it can get you *money* – or *things.*

Class I – Offences against the person	33,024
Class II – Burglary etc (ie offences against property with violence)	68,664
Class III – Theft (ie offences against property without violence)	**206,615**
Class IV – Malicious injuries to property	3,934
Class V – Offences against the currency	3,509
Class VI – Other offences not included	6,090
Indictable offences (all courts)	321,836

H.O. Criminal Statistics, 1971.

Draw your own conclusions. Society, apart from offering glittering prizes is also responsible for unemployment, low wages and lack of interesting jobs on leaving school.

This is not to excuse the crime, but we must try to understand it. Is the difference between *you*, who perhaps have given someone a ride on your crossbar, got off a bus without paying, seen an 'A' film without an adult with you, or grinned at dad's nerve when parking on a yellow line – and those who were punished simply that *they* were unlucky enough to be caught? Yet we base all our researches on 'criminals' from the small percentage who *are* caught, not from society as a whole!

Don't forget every crime is committed by a person who might *not* have committed it – if a combination of circumstances had been different! A man's character is the product of hereditary factors, background, upbringing, schooling, friendships, work possibilities and chances to love and be loved.

Having long ago abandoned the idea of pinning the criminal type by the shape of his head, the squareness of his ear or staring eyes – is it possible to describe the criminal by the 'type of crime'?

A friend of mine who is a prison visitor is adamant – 'My murderer isn't a criminal! He killed a man on reflex! The criminals are the professionals – the thieves who scorn the "gas-meter" type thief and only look at banks, large offices – nothing under £20,000!'
In 1971 motoring offences made up 58·5 per cent of all convictions in criminal courts. Could one of the major causes of crime be the invention of the internal combustion engine? The car is an outlet for aggression and anti-social behaviour and whilst it might seem unfair for a parking offence to end up in a

---

Talking point
Why *don't* the majority of us commit serious crimes, whereas we do commit minor ones?

Try listing the number of ways you have broken the law in the last week.

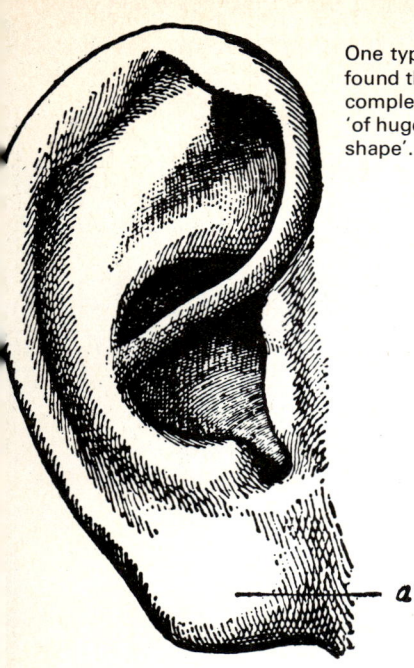

One type of criminal ear. Lombroso found that the lobe might be completely absent, or as in this case 'of huge dimensions and square in shape'.

In other words, if people, reasons and types of crime vary, why can't we accept that 'criminals' vary? Can law, which makes *generalized plans* for dealing with people's behaviour, cover all these varieties?

Criminal Statistics provide two very clear facts — crime is mostly the product of youth and masculinity. For in 1971, of the total number of persons found guilty in all courts, 277,308 (86·2 per cent) were male and 44,528 (13·8 per cent) were female; and 46 per cent of crimes were committed by people under twenty-one years of age! What might be the reasons for these differences?

criminal court this should certainly be the place for the hit-and-run driver, the drunkard at the wheel and the U-turner. Or should it?

Of course the persistent offender, the mentally abnormal, the 'hired' killer need to be studied, and treated, apart. But have they *anything* in common?

'The underpaid clerk who takes a subsidy from the firm's cash-box, meaning to put it back when he gets his wages at the end of the week, is far removed alike from the professional pickpocket, from the child who steals from a sweetshop for the devil of it, and from the compulsive stealer of women's underwear: yet all are guilty of larceny. Equally great is the distance between the mercy killer who gives an overdose to an incurable invalid, the exasperated husband who strangles a nagging wife after years of marital misery and the brutal murderer who bludgeons a man to death in order to rifle his savings.'

From *Crime and Criminal Law* by
Barbara Wootton

Can the punishments that law delivers be fair if each crime, criminal and court case is individual? Or will generalized treatments produce a 'criminal type'? Alexander Paterson, a man renowned for his interest in prison work, had this to say in 1906:

'It may be possible to visit a prison and discern a common type among a thousand captives, with their frequent obeisance and shifty eye, furtive mouth and slow-moving bodies. But it is prison life and not their criminality that has produced these attributes; the visitor has not discovered a criminal type, but the prisoner type, which is as old a phenomenon as the oldest walls men ever built. When first they enter a prison men are as different as the first hundred men stepping into a teashop on a given morning.'

From *Paterson on Prisons* by A. Paterson

Does the treatment itself aggravate the disease? Are we to punish the wicked or prevent the crime from recurring?

COME OFF IT!
At last: Jails get tough

PRISONER POWER!

YESTERDAY'S EXPRESS

By **JACK HILL** and **MAURICE TROWBRIDGE**

THE rebels of Britain's demo jails began to come to earth with a bang yesterday as governors doled out punishment and the Home Office switched to a sterner line.

It was Big Fizzer day on the Isle of Wight where governors at three prisons sat for hour after hour in their offices dealing with offenders.

At **ALBANY**, where protest riots sparked off the jails' crisis last week, the new get-tough line was emphasised by the transfer of two ringleaders to Wandsworth.

Albany's governor, Mr. Gifford Footer, faced with 433 charges involving 150 troublemakers, dealt with 60 men.

One will go before a board of visitors which can extend his sentence.

The other punishments ranged from a caution to 14 days' loss of remission.

Meanwhile, all of Albany's 363 prisoners will stay locked in their one-man cells until further notice.

ACTION

At the island's **CAMP HILL** jail a rooftop sit-in by 95 men ended in the afternoon after 24 hours.

As the rebels slithered down drainpipes a wall of officers was waiting to march each prisoner to the cells.

By then Governor Dennis Ward had already been in action, dealing with 187 other offenders.

Fifty-seven lost seven days' privileges, and 23 two days.

An officer at the jail said last night: "And that goes for Olympics on the telly as well."

At **PARKHURST** last night 24 men who began roof squatting on Monday afternoon were still there. But down below, governor Mr. Murdo Macleod gave 14 and 10 days' solitary to two men guilty of shouting abuse.

At **GARTREE**, Leicestershire, scene of a strike on Tuesday, the situation was almost back to normal and only 12 prisoners refused to work. Their ringleader was sentenced to seven days' loss of association, earnings, and privileges and the other 11, including Frankie Fraser, a member of the Richardson gang, were each fined 30p.

But 70 prisoners were last night still 60ft. up on the jail roof at **CHELMSFORD**, Essex, where £5,000 worth of damage was caused in a rampage through three blocks on Tuesday. The other 200 men were locked in the cells and all visits cancelled.

The biggest sit-in yet: Some of the 170 prisoners on the roof of Peterhead Jail in Aberdeenshire yesterday

PICTURE BY KEN LENNOX

Left: prisoners at Parkhurst. Is it just in the picture that they are faceless? The headline above voices a common opinion while the cartoon shows the prisoners' viewpoint. PROP, a prisoners' union, is aimed at improving conditions, but should prisoners have the right to protest?

'We're taking part in the sit-down all right — there's just no room to sit ...'

Prisons . . .

'Whether the prison is built on the starfish plan of Pentonville or consists of separate blocks with the yards and workshops between, as at Wormwood Scrubs, the interior of a prison hall is much the same. It suggests to the newcomer, at first glance, the hold of a great ship with the sky visible only through lights in the deck, far, far above. On each side are tiers of iron doors, the upper stories approached by steel and concrete landings, which overhang the central passageway and run its entire length. Between them are steel ladders which ascend from the centre of the hall and zig-zag up into the roof, their treads worn and their handrails burnished by countless generations of prisoners.

The cell doors, each divided from the next by a few feet of painted brickwork; the cold stone floor; the great wire net which is spread at first-floor level the whole length and breadth of the hall, proclaiming to all its grim purpose; the barred doors of the observation cells; and pervading everywhere the church-like silence and that indescribable prison smell, redolent with scrubbed boards and yellow soap, of leather and canvas and the sickly smell of beeswax, all combine to oppress the stranger with a sense of unrelenting strength and hardness, to instil in him the need for human relief within this fortress of stone and steel.'

From *Meet the Prisoner* by J. A. F. Watson

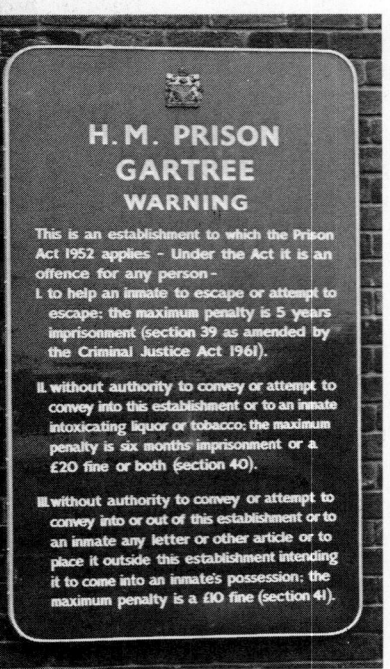

H. M. PRISON GARTREE
WARNING

This is an establishment to which the Prison Act 1952 applies – Under the Act it is an offence for any person –

l. to help an inmate to escape or attempt to escape: the maximum penalty is 5 years imprisonment (section 39 as amended by the Criminal Justice Act 1961).

ll. without authority to convey or attempt to convey into this establishment or to an inmate intoxicating liquor or tobacco: the maximum penalty is six months imprisonment or a £20 fine or both (section 40).

lll. without authority to convey or attempt to convey into or out of this establishment or to an inmate any letter or other article or to place it outside this establishment intending it to come into an inmate's possession: the maximum penalty is a £10 fine (section 41).

Subhumans of the Scrubs

This letter has been smuggled out of Wormwood Scrubs, where I am an inmate so I will not sign my name. My object is to draw to the attention of reasonably-minded people to the deplorable conditions in this establishment.

I am not writing out of self-pity or to cause trouble for the prison authorities. In fact I shall be discharged soon. I am writing in the interests of the health and welfare of an unfortunate section of society who must eventually rejoin the community. They must not come out in bad health and embittered because they have been treated like subhumans.

The prison is about 150 years old. Money recently allocated to improvements was spent on the wire perimeter fence. The food is unappetising and the actual portions are minute.

Work in the shops begins at 8 a.m. and with a luncheon break and exercise from 12 until 1.45 p.m. we work until 5 p.m. The last meal of the day at 5 o'clock is often a spoonful of jam and three slices of bread, and this has to last until 7 a.m. the next morning. The sanitary arrangements are primitive. Three water closets and two wash hand-basins for 140 men to use within the space of half an hour is usual.

The stipulated one hour's exercise each day is usually 15 minutes; when it is raining we have none. Bread and water in solitary confinement is still a popular punishment.

Most of us here would like to become useful members of society. But we get abuse and idle the days away. It boils down in the end to the fact that we all know we shall be coming back. What a wasteful and pitiful circle.

Inmate

Wormwood Scrubs

...and prisoners

The real, dramatic moment of truth in a court comes, not in Perry Mason-like climactic 'confessions' but when the judge, alone, pronounces sentence: the moment of *now, what to do with the man.* The moment when a man decides another man's life, when justice jostles with law, and compassion with precedent. Does the judge, now, treat the offender or the offence?

This is the moment, too, when we can judge whether the law is *preventive* or *punitive.* On the one hand you have the view of someone like former Lord Chief Justice Goddard — that the duty of criminal law is to punish and that the reformation of the prisoner is not the court's business; and on the other hand, this kind of view:

'The mood and temper of the public with regard to the treatment of crime and criminals is one of the most unfailing tests of the civilization of any country. We must not forget that when every material improvement has been effected in prisons, when the temperature has been rightly adjusted, when the proper food to maintain health and strength has been given, when the doctors, chaplains and prison visitors have come and gone, the convict stands deprived of everything that a free man calls life.'

Winston Churchill
From *Hansard,* 20 July 1910

But in both cases a man goes to prison. Of course times have changed from 1843 when Sarah Martin visited Yarmouth Gaol, a place 'filthy, confined, unhealthy and its occupants . . . infested with vermin and skin disease . . . where . . . the prisoners of both sexes, ranged from nine to eighty years old.' And we now replace learning passages from the Bible by rote with learning trades; and evening classes ranging from bird-spotting to modern languages and mathematics replace the inhuman pointlessness of stone-breaking. But women still pack spoons in Holloway and men, in many places, still sew mailbags.

Despite the lack of money to replace 'those great gaols of frozen ugliness' of Dartmoor and the Scrubs with newly designed prisons where the virtual impossibility of escape would allow the maximum freedom for the prisoners to live 'normal' lives inside, progress is being made.

Open prisons, parole systems, prisoner after-care and hostel schemes (the prisoner is prepared for 'after-life' by being allowed to have an outside job while returning to his prison-based hostel at night, his wages, apart from £1.50 are kept and given to him as a lump sum on release) begin to acknowledge that prisoners are diverse human beings, and, for the most part, like ourselves.

Leo Page in *Crime and The Community* points out 'they are often brave — a good burglar, for example, must of necessity be a man of nerve, courage and resource.'

If, as a former Lord of Appeal, Lord Simonds, believes, 'there remains in the courts a residual power to . . . conserve not only the safety but also the moral welfare of the state' — should this morality belong to the Old Testament 'an eye for an eye, and a tooth for a tooth' or to the Sermon on the Mount and forgiveness? Common law probably emerged in a Christian set of societies — yet it is a Christian society that gives us thirty years' imprisonment for the Great

Train Robbers (did the judge, because there was no *precedent* for the enormity of their takings, measure the strictness of their sentence by the enormity of their cheek?), three occupants to a cell, the liability of fourteen years' imprisonment for damaging cattle, but only six months for keeping a child in a brothel!

We are coming to the point where we have to ask 'what are prisons really for?' For punishment? As a deterrent? Then why do old prisoners come back, and why are crime figures rising? Are they to protect society from the 'few desperate men'? Then surely this is an argument, not for repression, but for devoting *more* time, money and skill to the problem of the few — *because they are few.*

The test of the penal system must lie in the question, 'What does society *do with a prisoner* once he's inside; and what are society's *reasons for doing* what it does.' Don't forget *we* are Society; *we* appoint the Governors.

There are those who feel that 'the defence of property' is more important than people; that 'Thou shalt not covet thy neighbour's house, thou shalt not covet thy neighbour's wife, nor his manservant, nor his maidservant, nor his ox, nor his ass, nor anything that is thy neighbour's' is more important than 'thou shalt not kill'.

No? Then why are some of the Great Train Robbers locked away for thirty years and a 'lifer' hardly ever serves more than ten?

BILL FLETCHER has spent only seven months out of prison in the last 30 years. All his sentences have been for petty thieving. The sum of his unlawful gains has been less than £40 in that period, during which it has cost the State around £31,000 to keep him locked up.

These facts came to light last week in a routine bulletin circu-

A SOCCER ROWDY PAYING THE PENALTY

Or what happened to a boy who took a strap to White Hart Lane

PETER THE Soccer rowdy never dreamed he would end up in a detention centre serving a three-month sentence.

" My dad thought I would be fined. I thought I would be banned from football matches for a year and was worrying about that," he said.

" The sentence I got was like being hit on the head."

Peter—not his real name—is no hooligan. But he imitated his pals and pulled a leather strap from an Underground train as he was on his way to the Spurs-Chelsea match at White Hart Lane on November 18.

He never saw the match. A policeman spotted the strap as he was queuing to enter the ground. A few days later Peter was at the Send junior detention centre in Surrey.

A detention centre is a severe place. It is meant to be. It is not brutal, but the boys sent there for three or six months can expect an organised life from before daybreak to lights-out.

It is physically tough and rather lonely.

Soccer rowdies, who are usually of previous good character, join hardened young thieves and car-joy-riders in a spartan regime which will certainly make them regret an afternoon's foolishness.

On parade at Send Detention Centre .. young thieves, joy-riders and a Soccer hooligan

REPORT BY MALCOLM STUART

The detention centre — for the young person a short, sharp punishment.

At first her husband may be on remand and he will be allowed a " closed " visit for 15 minutes every day. Some wives are so appalled by the conditions of the visit, sitting in a little booth with glass between them so they cannot touch nor sometimes even hear each other, with hysterical children trying to reach out to their fathers and a prison officer in the background, that they are put off returning. Others will do everything they can to visit every day, going without the bare necessities of life, even pawning their wedding rings, because by now they are having to scrape along on social security.

Later their husbands may be sent to prisons in other parts of the country, and there will be exhausting and expensive journeys with small children (for which they do not always get a travel warrant), long waits outside prisons in all weathers, no facilities for coping with children once inside, and only sketchy arrangements for refreshments.

Some places are worse than others, for instance on Dartmoor buses never seem to coincide with trains, but the exception to the general gloomy pattern is Winson Green prison, Birmingham, which has a wives' and families' centre outside the gates.

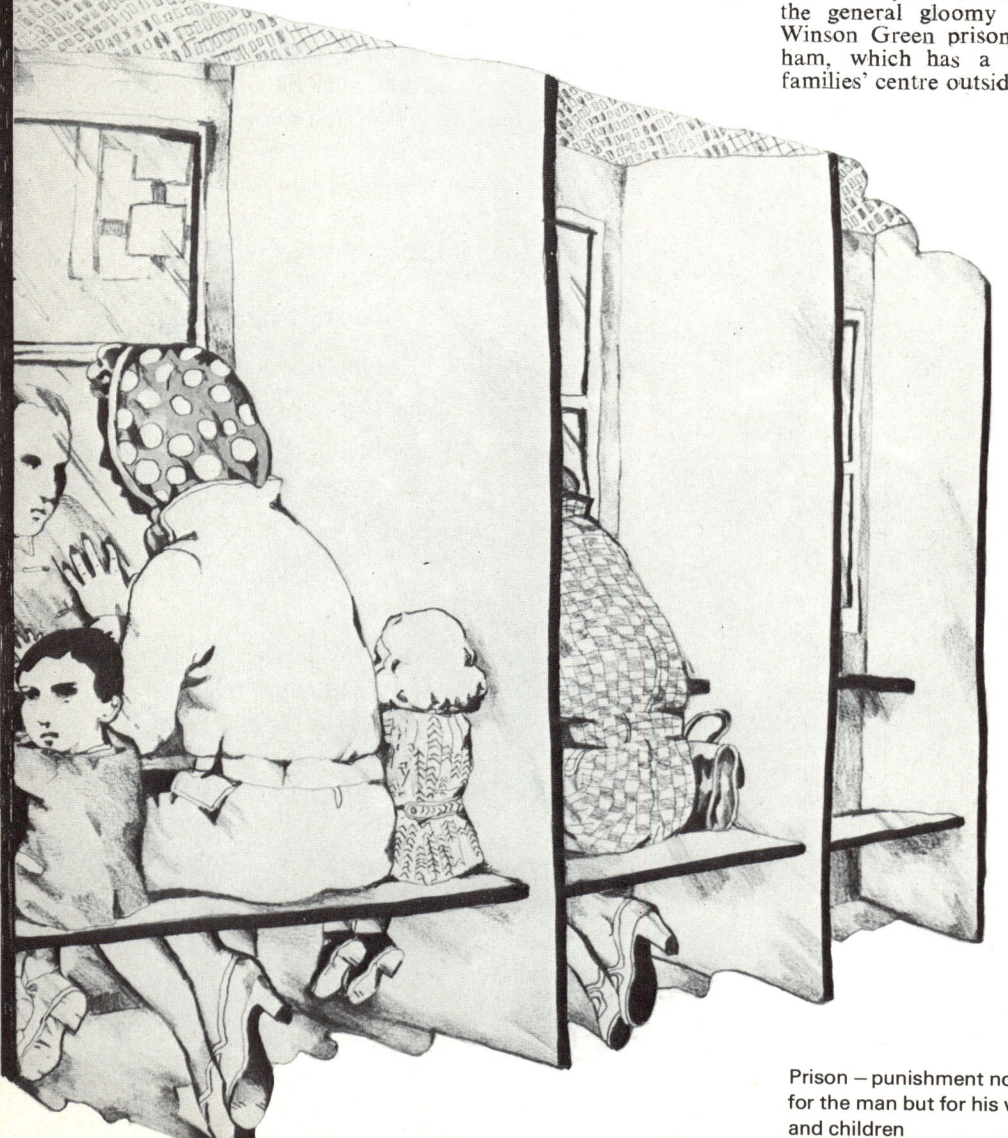

Prison — punishment not only for the man but for his wife and children

The lifer

Impressions of a prison visitor

What will he do? He will 'petition' his M.P., Governor, visiting V.I.P.s, everybody in sight, he will worry over time, food, the tannoy system, read books for hours and then not remember a single page or title, he will discuss and follow with the fanaticism of the single-minded any newspaper report or television programme or radio newsreel on any aspect that remotely concerns his condition — parole systems, hostel systems, visits, projected reconsiderations of new laws; his hair will fall out, his teeth go and maybe his eyes, he will hate visiting parties and concerts yet go to them; he will distrust the prison visitor but eventually ask for one — and then, sometimes with dignity, sometimes like a leech, he will come to depend overwhelmingly on them; he will seek a trade and find a million reasons or excuses for changing it or dropping it. He will masturbate and possibly flirt with homosexuality. He will, through the bush telegraph of the prison world, know and follow touchingly the fate of those who have 'gone down' and left while he stays on; he will be tired; occasionally he will refuse work, indeed lose precious 'remission' — all because he wants to withdraw from all contact with men — even his fellow prisoners; he will develop an acute sense of smell because prisoners don't smoke to excess or drink; the 'outside' will be bizarre, the 'inside' normal; elation will only come when he's 'given a date' — the date of his release. All else is waste.

Is welfare only for the under-seventeens?

Every routine action is watched.

No change

Although technically one can still be hanged for treason, setting fire to Her Majesty's shipyards or piracy with violence, many people also campaigned for the retention of the death penalty for the shooting of policemen or prison officers on the grounds that a 'free-for-all' could lead to the arming of the police 'for their own safety' and, more important, as one lobbyist put it, 'I've seen what happens to a man after *five* years — to his family, to his kids — to himself; death is *saner* than "life".'

But time doesn't always corrupt. What about a man who is *different* by the time he is to be punished from the man who committed the crime: for example, Caryl Chessman?

1921	**Born**
	Served various prison sentences
January 1948	**Accused of kidnapping two women with intent to rob with bodily harm**
	Kidnapping, in California, is punishable by death
July 1948	**Sentenced to death**

From July 1948 until May 1960, he survived seven execution dates by appeals. He wrote three books (*Cell 2455, Death Row* was a best-seller) about his prison life, educated himself slowly through the prison library and changed into an intelligent, reasonable and humane man. (Compare this with the attitudes and preoccupations of the two boy murderers in Truman Capote's book *In Cold Blood*.)

'Part of Chessman's plea for life was that during his years in prison he had become a different and better man, and there seems no reason to doubt that he had. The change in him is a tribute to the prison authorities. Just before his execution he wrote: "Now that the State has had its vengeance, I should like the world to consider what has been gained."'

From *Crime and Detection* by Julian Symons

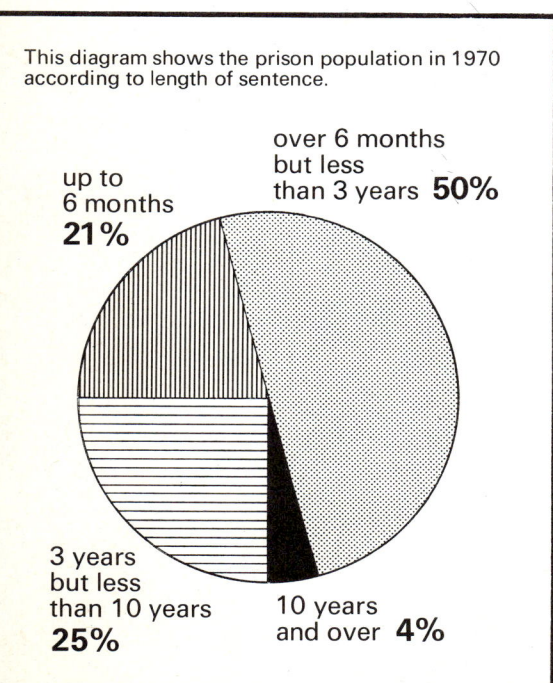

This diagram shows the prison population in 1970 according to length of sentence.

up to 6 months **21%**

over 6 months but less than 3 years **50%**

3 years but less than 10 years **25%**

10 years and over **4%**

May 1960

Executed in the gas chamber at San Quentin

CARYL CHESSMAN

The facts of the case

This is the only picture ever taken in a British Court of Justice showing a judge wearing the Black Cap, which is worn during the passing of a death sentence.

Under British Law, the lifer, having murdered, pays the supreme penalty the courts can impose now that capital punishment has been abolished. Presumably he has gone through the whole process of law — including the built-in sequences of appeals (see page 23). He can no longer be sentenced to life without any details of the crime being given in court as was Valentine Sokol at Leeds Assizes in March 1968 — just because he pleaded guilty.

Presumably too, like Polly, he would have been granted his fundamental rights in law: he would have been arrested properly, his statement given voluntarily with the police acting correctly (under the Judge's Rules which carefully regulate the conduct of the police because a few unguarded comments when first accused may damage his chances from the outset); and he would have been granted *legal aid* if he were broke and were committed for trial, or the 'interests of justice' so demanded it.

One hopes, too, that his trial would have taken place quickly because, as Sir John Waldron, Commissioner of the Metropolitan Police says, delays due to the legal system becoming clogged by the sheer numerical weight of cases and a shortage of judges, lawyers and courts, are disturbing — 'for it means that, with such a lapse of time, witnesses may not readily remember details'. And the legal process relies almost entirely on precision of evidence. And, unless he himself had wanted to put 'his character in issue' — the court need not have known if he had a bad character.

Because his wife is 'of one flesh', she couldn't have spoken against him; he could have remained silent throughout his trial — because the old common law stoutly maintained that no one can be compelled to incriminate himself. (But, as Jeremy Bentham pointed out, 'Innocence never takes advantage of it; innocence claims the right of speaking, as guilt invokes the privilege of silence.')

And, lastly, presumably the judge would have summed up meticulously, cleared away irrelevancies and guided the jury into their duty. Our lifer would have been convicted *on the facts of his particular case* — and no other; justice being done and being seen to be done. Indeed, so jealous is the law of its reputation for fairness that if, say, back in the original magistrates' court, the longhand 'depositions' had not been taken down properly, the whole case would have been thrown out — even though there was no fault in the trial itself!

But are the facts of the case the only considerations? The trial of the Rolling Stones might hint at other factors coming into play.

Private deeds and public words

On Sunday evening, 12 February 1967, police officers from West Sussex, acting on information received from the *News of the World,* entered the home of Keith Richards in West Wittering, Sussex, during a private house party and searched the house and all those present for drugs.

Three days later Mick Jagger was summoned under section one of the Drugs (Prevention of Misuse) Act, 1964, for having in his possession four tablets containing amphetamine sulphate and methyl amphetamine hydrochloride, drugs which belong to the 'soft' group. Keith Richards was summoned for alleged offences contrary to section 5(a) of the Dangerous Drugs Act, 1965, in allowing his house to be used for smoking cannabis resin.

In court, Jagger, asked what the tablets were for, said 'to stay awake and work', and his main defence was that he took them with the full approval of his doctor — although the doctor hadn't prescribed them. Judge Block ruled that the fact that the doctor agreed verbally to Jagger using them in an emergency was not the same as a prescription. Therefore Jagger's defence was useless. The jury found Jagger guilty in five minutes.

Jagger was returned to the court the next day handcuffed.

Richards' defence was that it was a private party and he thought someone had joined the party to notify the police; that, apart from the sweet sickly smell of incense in the room, as the police admitted, Richards 'behaved in a thoroughly adult manner'; Richards also said in evidence that he didn't know if anyone had

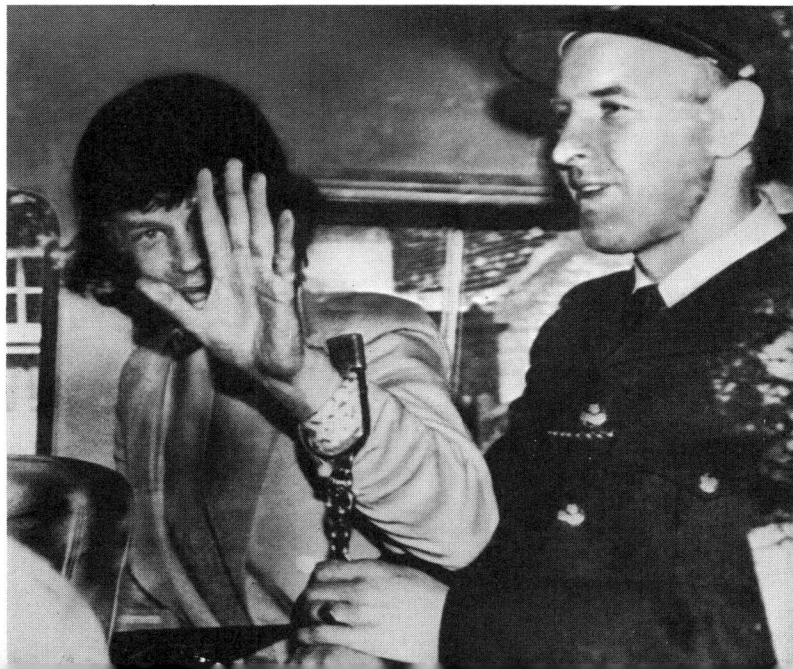

Mick Jagger remanded in custody.

Private deeds and public words

been smoking cannabis and would have objected had he known; nobody was delirious — 'they gave us every co-operation'. Judge Block in his summing up instructed the jury to ignore the nude lady, Richards' way of dress, and the fact that he was famous, and just to concentrate on whether it was satisfied cannabis resin was being smoked in the house.

He was found guilty.

Mr M. Havers, defence, in his final appeal pointed out — (a) over 150,000,000 of the type of tablets found on Jagger were prescribed annually on the National Health Service; (b) Jagger had surely been punished enough as a result of being photographed handcuffed and an ordinary man would not have suffered this publicity; (c) in the world of pop stars, temptations as well as pressures were great.

Richards was sentenced to one year's imprisonment and £500 costs (the maximum sentence in law is ten years); Jagger to three months' imprisonment (an uncommon sentence for first offenders) and £100 costs.

Both were released on bail of £7000 each.

Before the appeal court Richards' conviction was quashed and Jagger's reduced to conditional discharge by Lord Parker.

Police 'favour rich'

MR REG GALE, chairman of the Police Federation, said yesterday that the operation of the law certainly favoured the rich. He told a Liberal Party summer school at York that people with property tended to be considered more important than people without.

Mr Gale said it was part of the "feudal social system" that police would listen to complaints from "squire officialdom" rather than from poor people.

"If you misjudge your character and use the wrong sort of language to squire officialdom, they will complain and the police service takes note of these complaints," he said. Policemen were not good at judging the character of people with black skins.

Mr Gale said the rich man did not need to worry about the kind of car he had. The policeman was more likely to stop a youth on a scooter or a student in an old banger. There was more risk of breaking the law if one was poor. It might be because poor people did not have the education and did not realise they were committing an offence.

He blamed bad training, bad selection of intermediate officers, and the "crass ignorance of some senior officers," for the inability of the police to cope with today's social problems.

Who do the laws belong to?

In other words we are gradually arriving at a point where we have to acknowledge that the *law is fallible*; mistakes are made, not necessarily in the *facts* of law, but in *interpretation*.

Policemen, magistrates, judges are *servants of the law,* they must act within their rights and not overstep them. After all they are human and liable to be prejudiced. There is a world of difference between Lord Denning's observation, 'I have always held the view that in court any judge or magistrate when he sits to try a case is himself on trial' and the over-zealous policeman who is only a sliver away from the provoker. Law-makers, naturally, are aware of possible error; that is why safeguards such as the appeals machinery (onus on the prosecution, and strict rules over what is and what is not admissible evidence) exist. Compulsory training for lay magistrates is now planned; special police powers are zealously scrutinized; there is even talk of taking the *sentencing* out of the hands of judges. In the meantime *sentencing exercises,* where judges 'try' identical test-trials, are being tried out to produce uniformity of sentencing.

A coloured man is walking, late at night, carrying a transistor radio . . .

Policeman Hey!

Man Yes, man?

Policeman What you got there?

Man Nothing!

Policeman Name and address?

Man Why, what you want it for, man?

Policeman Don't 'man' me. Name and address?

Man What gives you the right to ask me for my name and address?

Policeman Name and address?

Man Get off me, man!

He touches the policeman, who, expecting assault, retaliates . . .
Now,
(a) This is a situation where *there is a mutual expectation of aggression*: the coloured man doesn't know the policeman has the right to arrest on reasonable suspicion (being in unlawful possession of the transistor) and so is entitled to ask for a name and address, and *doesn't have to explain why he wants them*; on the other hand the policeman *knows* he doesn't have to give an explanation.
(b) A more serious offence — assault on a police officer — arises than would have been necessary had *both* known about each other's rights and powers.
(c) Yet, if the policeman had been over-polite, and the transistor had been stolen, arrest might have been more difficult!

Law, more often than not, is a question of education.

Who do the laws belong to?

Of course 'justice' can never now be as rough as this case of pick-pocketing in the mid-nineteenth century (from Sir Henry Hawkins' *Memoires*):

'The accused having "held up his hand", and the jury having solemnly sworn to hearken to the evidence . . . the witness for the prosecution climbs into the box, which was like a pulpit, and, before he has time to look around and see where the voice comes from, he is examined as follows by the prosecuting counsel:

"I think you were walking up Ludgate Hill on Thursday 25th about half past two in the afternoon, and suddenly felt a tug at your pocket and missed your handkerchief, which the constable now produces. Is that it?"[1]

1   These are all 'leading questions', i.e. they are questions which *demand* let alone *suggest* the answer yes, and would not nowadays be allowed.

"Yes sir."
"I suppose you have nothing to ask him?" says the judge. "Next witness."[2, 3]

2   Note that the accused is *not* represented: now legal aid is free.
3   The judge should never indicate that *there is no case*; the judge should be neutral.

Constable stands up.
"Were you following the prosecutor on this occasion when he was robbed on Ludgate Hill? and did you see the prisoner put his hand into the prosecutor's pocket and take this handkerchief out of it?"[4]

4   More than one question is being asked at the same time; they should be separate and free from suggestion, e.g. Were you followed? *Answer.*
Did anything happen? *Answer.*
What did happen? etc.

"Yes sir."
Judge to prisoner: "Nothing to say, I suppose?"
Then to the jury: "Gentlemen, I suppose you have no doubt? I have none."[5, 6, 7]

5   Here the trial should have switched from the case of the prosecution to the case for the defence. Here the judge should invite the prisoner either to give evidence on oath or make a statement from the dock and give him an opportunity to call witnesses.
6   The duty of the judge at the end of the defence case is to tell the jury what the law is and he may then, to help the jury, sum up the evidence given on *both* sides.
7   The judge should not express an opinion. All matters for the jury are *fact*, the judge just provides the *law*.

Jury: "Guilty, my lord," as though to oblige his lordship.[8]

8   The jury would normally retire to consider the evidence.

Judge to prisoner: "Jones we have met before — we shall not meet again for some time — seven years' transportation. Next case."[9, 10]

9   Before sentencing anyone to prison nowadays, a judge will normally ask for a Social Inquiry Report.
10   Seven years for stealing a hankie!

Time: two minutes, fifty-three seconds.'[11]

11   It is impossible to get through *any* modern jury trial in under *an hour*!

Poor Old Jones! It's a remarkable fact that before 1898 no defendant in a criminal trial had the right to give evidence for himself. He couldn't even say, 'I'm not guilty, m'lud'!

'If I've granted *him* a decree nisi, then who did I just sentence to life imprisonment in court five?'

1,500-year gaol term

An all-white jury in Oklahoma City yesterday convicted a Negro, aged 22, of raping a white employee of a telephone company on Thursday. They sentenced him to 1,500 years in prison after the prosecution said that 500 years would be just a slap on the wrist.

Judges are not infallible. When sentencing they have, almost always, a choice between maximum and minimum sentences — and what if they don't like long hair, student demonstrators or pop singers — let alone gifted train robbers? The way they deal with such offenders then reveals THEIR prejudices, not necessarily those of the rest of us. More often than not judges belong to a closed, select class which is far removed from the world of Alan, Polly, The Lifer or an immigrant.

Judges do not invent laws but, as we have seen, base their judgments on *precedents* or past cases. In this way law is *backward looking* and the standards of a past age are used as rules for the present. Law changes slowly and can sometimes be accused of being 'wrong' when what is really meant is that it's out of tune with what people think.

Although we no longer accuse old ladies living alone of witchcraft, until recently we did *according to the law as it stood* punish homosexuals living together. Society's views on homosexuality changed and the law had to change too. Law and morality are seldom in tune but this is not too bad as long as we realize that *law is not infallible*: that it can, and must, change. Law must belong to the society it governs, to you, to me, otherwise it will rest purely in the hands of those who have the power to make it — an undemocratic and dangerous power.

Talking point
Should a judge be allowed to drive a car? If *yes*, he might crash and then would be seen to be fallible. If *no* — how does he know 'how the other half lives'? By catching a bus? But he probably travels by taxi! But we don't want him infallible, we want him to be human. But if he is human, and therefore capable of error, remember he holds a job where people might suffer greatly because of his errors . . .
CONTINUE!

Lord Hodson fined—careless driving

Lord Hodson (75), former Lord of Appeal, was fined £75 at Henley, Oxon, today for driving without due care and attention.

The case followed an accident near Henley, in which a woman died.

The magistrates did not disqualify Lord Hodson because of his wonderful record.

Would you break the law for an ideal?

Demonstration: Prague

Police attack: Ulster

Police attack: South Africa

Retaliation: London

Things are getting better . . .

'I sup with my friend; I cannot return to my home, not even in my chariot, without danger of a pistol being clapt to my breast. I build an elegant villa, ten or twenty miles distant from the capital; I am obliged to provide an armed force to convey me thither, lest I should be attacked on the road with fire and ball.'

Jonas Hanway, 1775

'In Boston, office girls refuse to work alone after six. In Kansas City, hospitals have trouble finding night nurses. Prudent Chicagoans try not to ride the el [elevated railway] after dark, and attendance at White Sox games is down, not merely because of the team's poor record. Nearly everywhere, often without even consciously thinking about it, city dwellers are adjusting their lives, their residences and their jobs to the fear of physical violence. Parks that once were playgrounds on hot summer nights are now virtually empty. Iron bars and heavy mesh cover exposed windows, while doors are double- and triple-locked.'

Time, 19 July 1968

. . . or are they?

Project
Why not make up your own series of questions on the police, crime, prisons, and young offenders, and ask representatives from the various age groups in *your area* to give their opinions: then put them all together. Don't be surprised at the results — exactly half the voters of all ages and of both sexes thought the sentence on Mick Jagger should have been longer, 30 per cent about right, and only 14 per cent too severe!

Talking point
What effects do you imagine the following have on crime?
1   The invention of gunpowder
2   The payment of police
3   Street lighting
4   Employment in factories
5   The creation of detectives
6   War
7   The discovery of fingerprints
8   Cars
9   The colour of a man's skin
10   The welfare state

TV crime is imitated

FROM OUR OWN CORRESPONDENT
Moscow, June 16

A psychopath armed with a rifle and knives tried to " recreate " the tragedy at Austin, Texas, two years ago when a young American shot 14 people dead and wounded about 30 in a fusillade from a university tower.

According to General Schelokov, the head of the new Ministry for Social Order here, an outpatient at a Russian psychiatric clinic installed himself with his weapons on a balcony overlooking a busy street a week after Soviet television had screened a documentary newsreel about the Texan killer's rampage.

That the average American between his second and sixty-fifth year spends 3,000 entire days (nearly nine years of his life) simply sitting watching TV ;

That by the time a five-year-old child in the United States enters kindergarten, he has already spent more time learning about the world from the family TV set than is spent by a BA student in a classroom throughout his college years ;

That what both the adult and the child are watching all this time are programmes containing (according to a recent average week) an incident of violence every 14 minutes and a killing every three-quarters of an hour.

These staggering facts have emerged from evidence presented to the National Commission on the Causes and Prevention of Violence at a public hearing on Capitol Hill. The heads of all three major

The mask of evil

On my wall hangs a Japanese carving,
The mask of an evil demon, decorated
   with gold lacquer.
Sympathetically I observe
The swollen veins of the forehead,
   indicating
What a strain it is to be evil.

Bertolt Brecht
Translated by H. R. Hays

In the meantime

If we accept that the more complex our society becomes, the more laws seem necessary, how can we safeguard *ourselves* when, in exchange for all the benefits, we are liable to lose even more and more of our freedom?

The obvious answer is that we must see to it that the laws are as *fair* as possible; that the individual is not forgotten; that the way laws deal with people should be preventive rather than vindictive.

But when we congratulate ourselves on the fact that roughly 50 per cent of those who go to borstal, prison, etc., do benefit, and like the 70 per cent of first offenders, don't reappear before the courts – we are still left with a plum question:

Talking point
Can it ever be *right* that crime should go unpunished?

To the criminal the law is a muddle, without principle or consistency – and the reason for the muddle is that the punishment is never proportional to the crime. But where he can grudgingly *feel* sense in law is when the welfare side of law is allowed to operate; when a trust is put in him – as in hostel schemes, remission, parole and probation.

(Even a good idea like the new parole scheme, however, can have inhuman twists – on 1 April 1968, 4764 prisoners were eligible for release; only 350 were released. As one prisoner put it:

'I can't describe to you what it's like, this parole system. The only thing is that when you get up at half past five and pack your things, you know the others are looking at you and saying to themselves, "Why's he going out and not me? Same sentence, same circumstances, why haven't they accepted me?" It's the only topic of conversation. They'll have to do something about the others as quick as they can.')

If we presume that nobody – except perhaps the wronged person – really wants *pain* to be a part of punishment (those who think they believe in birching and flogging should read first-hand accounts of the results of such punishments), then we are left with the one constant, understandable 'thread of welfare' running through the entire system – probation.

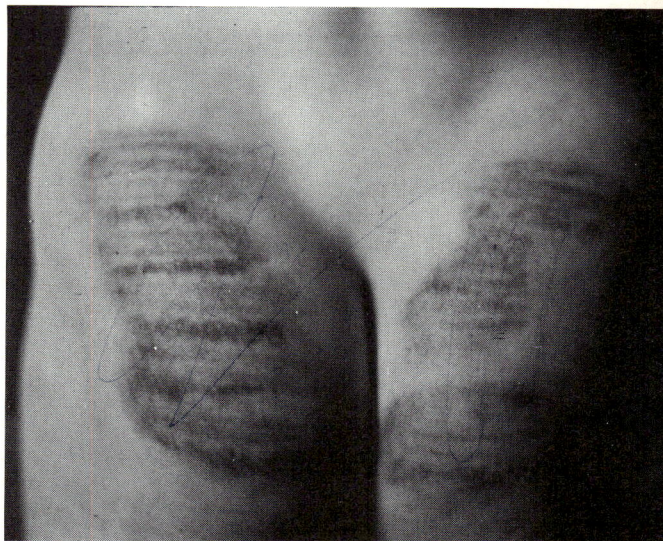

This photograph shows the bottom of a boy who had been punished for smoking at Court Lees Approved School, 1968.

For them I say the birch and the birch and the birch again. I cannot abide savagery, and those who indulge in it should pay the full price. – Lord Arran in *Evening News*

Probation

Probation is now a form of adult treatment:
Supervision (see page 6) which may be by a
Probation Officer, is reserved for juveniles. It's
still not being 'let off' — it goes down on your
record for life!

Adults placed under a Probation Order still
have to satisfy certain conditions — i.e. Probation
is only considered as a possibility and is rejected
if it cannot be applied, it is the result of elaborate
inquiries, the offender must agree to cooperate,
to work hard, behave himself, keep away from
'dangerous areas', if Probation is broken the
penalties are severe (yet in 1967, 29,694 people
on probation appeared before the court for a
fresh offence or a breach of a probation order)
and he must have somewhere to live.

Now, in the case of juveniles, although not
inserted as requirements of the order, the aim of
the supervision is the same — i.e. establishment
of regular work and school attendance
with the cooperation of the offender.

Can the order help Polly?

It's a sad but inescapable fact that neither the
professional nor the 'specialist' type of offender
can ever be expected to respond to probation —
especially the latter, who repeats his one ability
ad nauseam — the smash-and-grab thief, the
bogus estate agent, the flannel-foot burglar who
chooses the same dogless houses time after
time, the phoney meter-reader or window
cleaner; in a sense the stupid, predictable
offender.

Polly is none of these. Can a system that
has been in operation for sixty years help her . . . ?

Meet Miss Knight

Like most probation officers under thirty, Miss Knight is a graduate, with a specialized diploma; she is quiet-spoken, and, with a case-load of fifty-five, overworked. Besides dealing with people on probation she must prepare court reports on people convicted, supervise the after-care of people discharged from penal institutions, travel about, and sit in court.

Question Everyone is presumed innocent until proved guilty – but if you start investigating an offender's circumstances and history *before sentence* – aren't you anticipating the verdict?

Miss Knight Ha! Don't forget everybody, including the offender, has to agree to it. Most juveniles plead guilty. I'm here to 'advise, assist and befriend' – not to judge.

Question It's unusual to get supervision first time, isn't it?

Miss Knight For the 'slip' of the first offence it makes more sense to fine or give conditional discharge: Supervision on the second offence reminds them that it might be the beginning of a trend.

Question Then why did Polly get supervision?

Miss Knight It's attitude and, unfortunately, not only Polly's attitude.

Question What was her attitude first time she visited you?

Miss Knight She came in and sat with her back to me.

Question What did you do?

Miss Knight I could have said, 'Turn round, sit up and listen!' But I just sat there. Then she turned round. I said, 'Did you find it hard getting here?' Silence. 'You must hate the court?' She burst into tears.

Meet
Miss Knight

Question Did you take notes?

Miss Knight No. If I did she'd assume I'm 'part of the court', as she would if I was a uniformed constable.

Question Did she accept you were trying to help?

Miss Knight In time. *She* must see *she* needs help, and perhaps her parents.

Question Were they hostile?

Miss Knight The very fact that I go into their home must imply, to them, that they're bad parents. I have to accept they think me a busy-body as part of my job.

Question What is your job?

Miss Knight To help people; to listen — to both sides; to build up trust. Most of the problems we deal with are failures in communication.

Question Do you tell Mrs Waters, say, what Polly thinks — and vice versa?

Miss Knight Never.

Question You must feel tempted?

Miss Knight The greatest danger is to side only with the child.

Question What *is* Polly's problem?

Miss Knight *(reluctantly)* It's partly a home problem. The first real clue we had to the difficulties was the fact that Mr Waters wouldn't attend court. He's a night-worker in the print and has been for years. He had to get his sleep. It's 'harmless' nerve ends like that that build up to . . . trouble.

Question Are they happy?

Miss Knight Who is! It took a lot for Mrs Waters to admit this. She's a terribly bottled-up person because she's lonely. She was *physically* disgusted at having to go to court. It's not only in slums that things are thrown, you know. Mr Waters doesn't throw anything except silence. He hates what he calls his wife's 'snobbery' — her need to live in better and better areas. He couldn't care less. They

moved house so that Polly could get into a 'better' grammar school — uprooting her from her old friends.

Question   Couldn't you just point this out to Polly?

Miss Knight   Wouldn't it be better if she pointed it out to me?

Question   Has she?

Miss Knight   Yes . . . but it's taken time.

Question   All this 'home' problem seems a cliché — very pat. What about the school report?

Miss Knight   Again there was the clue that she'd gone *suddenly* down hill.

Question   A boy friend?

Miss Knight   *(laughing)* Yes — again very pat — eh? It took her three months to admit him to me. She's *still* terrified her mother won't like him, and because she's in a new school she's few friends to confide in there. The second jumper she took was blue — Brian likes blue!

Question   If Polly's to benefit from supervision — presumably you've got to 'bring the two sides together'?

Miss Knight   Polly's my first concern. If we can go on talking — I'm her only confidante now, remember — then things'll improve. If she can be *objective* about herself, the boy, her mother, school and the pressure of supervision — then we'll win. But to be objective is pretty adult.

Question   Is she objective?

Miss Knight   I'm thirty and I find it hard. She's only just fifteen.

Question   Do you ever feel things are hopeless?

Miss Knight   Fifty—fifty.

Question   Do you feel you can cope?

Miss Knight   I know *I'm* fallible. I know I can't do everything — who can! To judge is to kill. I like to think it's me, and the law's on probation — not only Polly and the other fifty-four.

'If this man were your father —
what would you feel?'

'If this man asked for a job,
would you employ him?'

'If this were *you*, what would
you think of society?'